HA

JA
BUSINESS
MANAGEMENT
DICTIONARY

HARRAP

JAPANESE BUSINESS MANAGEMENT DICTIONARY

Hajime Takamizawa

Professor of Japanese
Showa Women's University, Tokyo

James Coveney

Emeritus Professor of Modern Languages
University of Bath

HARRAP

First published in Great Britain 1999
by Chambers Harrap Publishers Ltd
7 Hopetoun Crescent, Edinburgh EH7 4AY

ISBN 0245 60662 9

Printed in Great Britain by Clays Ltd, St Ives plc

目　次
Contents

Introduction

The rapid growth of the management sciences has resulted in the coining of many terms to describe new techniques and concepts, terms which are not easily found in current English-Japanese and Japanese-English dictionaries. A dictionary of business management terms is therefore needed by both business practitioners and by students of business administration.

Our dictionary is an attempt to fill this gap. The terms included have been drawn from the main areas of business management interest: business policy and corporate planning, finance, information technology, marketing, operational research, personnel management, and production.

We have tried to keep a proper balance by not overemphasizing any one area. Moreover, since the scope of the subject is very wide, we have selected only those terms in most frequent use.

We wish to thank the staff of the Tokyo office of McKinsey and Company, Inc. who have contributed considerably to the dictionary with advice and suggestions. We are also most grateful to the Great Britain-Sasakawa Foundation and to the Daiwa Anglo-Japanese Foundation for generous financial assistance which enabled us to meet in Japan. Finally, we should like to thank Mr Yasuo Kitaoka, President, International Communications, Inc., Tokyo, for helpful advice in connection with publication of the dictionary.

Hajime Takamizawa
James Coveney

はじめに

経営学の発展に伴って、先端技術や新しい経営の概念を表す語彙が急増しています。本辞典は、経営、事業計画、金融、情報工学、販売、業務調査、人事管理、生産など、経営管理に関わる新しい用語を幅広く収録した、最新のビジネス英和・和英辞典です。

編纂にあたっては、各分野の新語を使用頻度の高いものからバランスよく選定しました。用語の選定にあたって貴重な助言を与えて下さいましたマッケンジー・ジャパン社のスタッフの方々や研究費の助成をいただきました英国笹川基金、大和日英基金に感謝の意を表するとともに、出版に際して多大な御協力をいただきました国際コミュニケーションズ代表取締役社長、北岡靖男氏に心からお礼申し上げます。

高見澤 孟
ジェームズ・コヴネイ

本辞典の使い方

本辞典は英和辞典と和英辞典を一冊にまとめ、利用者が十分活用できるように構成されています。

英和辞典では、日本語の意味とともにその読みをローマ字で併記し、また和英辞典では、見出し語をローマ字で表記していますので、日本人だけではなく外国人の方々にも、気軽に使っていただけます。

英和辞典と和英辞典はともに、単語、連語に関わらず、すべての見出し語をアルファベット順に配列しています。そのため連語の場合も、基本的には前に置かれた単語から引くことになります。

ただし英和辞典では、利用者の便宜を図るため、単語の見出しの下に、その単語が中に含まれている連語を斜体で列記しています。つまり、連語の意味を後ろに置かれた単語でも引くことができるため、素早く目的の語句を見つけ出すことができます。あるキーワードの含まれた連語を検索するときなどに、また、うろ覚えの連語の意味を調べるときなどにも活用することができます。

ENGLISH-JAPANESE

A

abandonment:
product abandonment seisan-chūshi 生産中止
ability nōryoku 能力
ability to compete kyōsō-ryoku 競争力
ability to pay shiharai-nōryoku 支払い能力
above par gakumen-ijō 額面以上
absenteeism keikakuteki kekkin 計画的欠勤
absorption costing gappei-hiyō 合併費用
acceptance:
brand acceptance burando ni taisuru ninki ブランドに対する人気
consumer acceptance tokuisaki-hikiuke-tegata 得意先引受手形
access *v.* sannyū-suru 参入する
access:
multi access tajū-shori 多重処理
random access randamu-akusesu ランダムアクセス
accountability kekka ni taishite oubeki gimu 結果に対して負うべき義務
accountables kaikei-sekinin 会計責任
accountant:
chief accountant kaikei sekinin-sha 会計責任者
accounting keiri 経理
cost accounting genka-keisan 原価計算
creative accounting chōbo-sōsa 帳簿操作
management accounting kanri-kaikei 管理会計
profit centre accounting rieki-tan'i-bumon-kaikei 利益単位部門会計
responsibility accounting sekinin-kaikei 責任会計
accounting department keiribu 経理部
accounting model kaikei-moderu 会計モデル
accounting period kaikei-kikan 会計期間
accounting ratio kaikei-hiritsu 会計比率
accounts:
consolidated accounts renketsu-kessan 連結決算
group accounts sōgō-zaimu-hyō 総合財務表
acquire *v.* kakutoku-suru 獲得する
acquisition shutoku 取得
data acquisition dētā-shutoku データー取得
acquisition profile shutoku-jōkyō 取得状況
acquisitions kakutoku 獲得
across-the-board increase ichiritsu-shōkyū 一律昇給
action:
industrial action sangyō-katsudō 産業活動
unofficial action hi-kōnin-katsudō 非公認活動
action plan kōdō-hōshin 行動方針
actionable soshō no taishō to

naru 訴訟の対象となる
activate *v.* kasseika-suru 活性化する
active market kōkyō-shijō 好況市場
activity:
support activity shien-katsudō 支援活動
activity chart gyōmu-hyō 業務表
activity sampling katsudō-chūshutsu (-chōsa) 活動抽出(調査)
actualization:
self-actualization jiko-hyōgen 自己表現
adaptive control tekiōsei-kanri 適応性管理
add-on equipment ado'on-setsubi アドオン設備
added:
value added fuka-kachi 付加価値
value added tax (VAT) fukakachi-zei 付加価値税
adequacy:
capital adequacy shihon-datōsei 資本妥当性
administration kanri 管理
financial administration zaimu-kanri 財務管理
administration-production ratio kanri-keiei-hiritsu 管理経営比率
administrative ability keieinōryoku 経営能力
administrative control keiei-kanri-hōhō 経営管理方法
administrative cost kanrihi 管理費
administrative overheads kanri-shokeihi 管理諸経費
administrative theory keiei-riron 経営理論
ADP (automatic data processing) jidō-dētā-shori 自動データー処理
advancement:
executive advancement kanrishoku no shōshin 管理職の昇進
advantage:
competitive advantage kyōsō-jō no yūi 競争上の優位
advertising:
corporate advertising kyōdō-kōkoku 共同広告
subliminal advertising mijikai komāsharu-messōji 短いコマーシャルメッセージ
advertising agent kōkoku-dairiten 広告代理店
advertising appropriation senden-hiyō 宣伝費用
advertising budget senden-yosan 宣伝予算
advertising campaign senden-sen 宣伝戦
advertising drive senden-katsudō 宣伝活動
advertising effectiveness senden-kōka 宣伝効果
advertising manager senden-tantōsha 宣伝担当者
advertising media senden-baitai 宣伝媒体
advertising message senden-bun 宣伝文
advertising research kōkoku-chōsa 広告調査
advertising theme kōkoku no shudai 広告の主題
advisory services komon-gyōmu 顧問業務

affiliate company kogaisha 子会社
after-sales service afutā-sābisu アフターサービス
after-tax profit zeibiki-rieki 税引き利益
agency dairiten 代理店
agenda:
hidden agenda kakusareta-gidai 隠された議題
to be on the agenda gidai ni ireru 議題に入れる
agent:
advertising agent kōkoku-dairiten 広告代理店
sole agent sō-dairiten 総代理店
agreement kyōtei 協定
collective bargaining agreement dantai-rōdō-kyōyaku 団体労働協約
gentleman's agreement shinshi-kyōtei 紳士協定
productivity agreement seisansei-kyōyaku 生産性協約
algorithm sanpō 算法
alliance:
strategic alliance senryaku-teki-dōmei (-kankei) 戦略的同盟（関係）
allocate *v.* warifuru 割り振る
allocation:
resource allocation shigen-haibun 資源配分
allocation of costs hiyō-haibun 費用配分
allocation of responsibilities sekinin-buntan 責任分担
allotment:
budget allotment yosan-haibun 予算配分
allowance:
capital allowance shihon-hikiatekin 資本引当金
depreciation allowance genka-shōkyaku-hikiatekin 減価償却引当金
amalgamate *v.* gōdō-suru 合同する
amalgamation gappei 合併
analog(ue) computer anarogu-konpyūta アナログコンピュータ
analog(ue) representation anarogu-kigō アナログ記号
analysis:
break-even analysis son'eki-bunki-bunseki 損益分岐分析
competitor analysis kyōsō-kankei-bunseki 競争関係分析
contribution analysis kōkendo-bunseki 貢献度分析
cost analysis hiyō-bunseki 費用分析
cost-benefit analysis (CBA) hiyōkōka-bunseki 費用効果分析
cost-volume-profit analysis son'eki-bunseki 損益分析
critical path analysis (CPA) rinkai-keiro-bunseki 臨界経路分析
decision analysis hantei-bunseki 判定分析
depth analysis shindo-bunseki 深度分析
environmental analysis kankyō-bunseki 環境分析
financial analysis zaimu-bunseki 財務分析
input-output analysis tōnyū-sanshutsu-bunseki 投入

産出分析
investment analysis tōshi-bunseki 投資分析
job analysis shokumu-bunseki 職務分析
marginal analysis genkai-bunseki 限界分析
media analysis baitai-bunseki 媒体分析
morphological analysis keitai-bunseki 形態分析
multiple regression analysis (MRA) chikuji-tajū-kaiki-bunseki 逐次多重回帰分析
needs analysis nīzu-bunseki ニーズ分析
network analysis netto-wāku-bunseki ネットワーク分析
overhead value analysis (OVA) sōkeihi-kachi-bunseki 総経費価値分析
problem analysis mondai-bunseki 問題分析
product analysis seihin-bunseki 製品分析
profit-factor analysis rieki-yōin-bunseki 利益要因分析
profitability analysis shūekisei-bunseki 収益性分析
project analysis kikaku-bunseki 企画分析
quantitative analysis keiryō-bunseki 計量分析
regression analysis kaiki-bunseki 回帰分析
risk analysis kiken-bunseki 危険分析
sales analysis uriage-bunseki 売上分析
sensitivity analysis kando-bunseki 感度分析
sequential analysis chikuji-bunseki 逐次分析
skills analysis ginō-bunseki 技能分析
social analysis shakai-bunseki 社会分析
systems analysis shisutemu-bunseki システム分析
training needs analysis kunren-nīzu-bunseki 訓練ニーズ分析
transactional analysis (TA) kōryū-bunseki 交流分析
value analysis (VA) kachi-bunseki 価値分析
variance analysis bunsan-bunseki 分散分析

analytical training bunseki-kunren 分析訓練

ancillary operations hojoteki-sagyō 補助的作業

answerback code ōtō-kigō 応答記号

answerphone rusuban-denwa 留守番電話

anticipatory response mikomi-kaitō 見込回答

appeal:
sales appeal hanbai-apīru 販売アピール

application:
software application sofutouea-tekiyō-gyōmu ソフトウエア適用業務

apportion *v.* wariateru 割り当てる

apportionment haibun 配分

appraisal satei 査定
capital appraisal shihon-

satei 資本査定
capital expenditure appraisal shiharai-shihon-satei 支払資本査定
financial appraisal zaimu-satei 財務査定
investment appraisal tōshi-satei 投資査定
market appraisal shijō-hyōka 市場評価
performance appraisal gyōseki-satei 業績査定
self appraisal jiko-satei 自己査定
staff appraisal shokuin hyōka 職員評価

appraise *v.* satei-suru 査定する
appreciate *v.* hyōka-suru 評価する
appreciation seitō na hyōka 正当な評価
approach:
functional approach kinō-bunseki 機能分析
systems approach shisutemu-apurōchi システムアプローチ
top management approach saikō-keieisha-hōshiki 最高経営者方式

appropriate *v.* wariateru 割り当てる
appropriation:
advertising appropriation kōkoku-hiyō 広告費用
budget appropriation yosan-wariate 予算割当
marketing appropriation ryūtsū-keihi 流通経費

approval:
functional approval kinōteki-kakunin 機能的確認

aptitude test nōryoku-shiken 能力試験
arbitrage kawase-saitei 為替裁定
arbitrage stock sayatori-kabu さや取り株
arbitrageur sayatori-gyōsha さや取り業者
arbitration chūsai, saitei 仲裁、裁定
area:
growth area seichō-chi'iki 成長地域
problem area mondai-ryōiki 問題領域
product area seihin-han'i 製品範囲
sales area hanbai-chiiki 販売地域
trading area shōken 商圏

area manager chiiki-sekininsha 地域責任者
area network:
wide area network (WAN) kōiki-nettowāku 広域ネットワーク

arm's length kengen-han'i 権限範囲
artificial intelligence jinkō-chinō 人工知能
assembly line nagare-sagyō 流れ作業
assess *v.* satei-suru 査定する
assessment satei 査定
demand assessment juyō-satei 需要査定
project assessment purojekuto-hyōka プロジェクト評価
quality assessment hinshitsu-hyōka 品質評価
risk assessment kiken-satei

危険査定
assessment centre satei-sentā 査定センター
asset liability management fusai-kanri 負債管理
asset management shisan-kanri 資産管理
asset portfolio shisan-meisai-hyō 資産明細表
asset-stripping shisan-hōshutsu 資産放出
asset turnover shisan-kaiten (ritsu) 資産回転（率）
asset value shisan-kachi 資産価値
assets shisan 資産
  capital assets kotei-shisan 固定資産
  current assets ryūdō-shisan 流動資産
  earnings on assets shūeki-shisan 収益資産
  fixed assets kotei-shisan 固定資産
  hidden assets kakushi-shisan 隠し資産
  intangible assets mukei-shisan 無形資産
  liquid assets ryūdō-shisan 流動資産
  net assets jun-shisan 純資産
  net current assets jun-ryūdō-shisan 純流動資産
  quick assets tōza-shisan 当座資産
  revaluation of assets shisan-saihyōka 資産再評価
  tangible assets yūkei-shisan 有形資産
  wasting assets genmō-shisan 減耗資産
assignment:
  job assignment ninmu 任務
assistant:
  line assistant kōjō-jichō 工場次長
  staff assistant hosa-sei 補佐制
assistant manager fuku-shihainin 副支配人
assistant to manager shihai-nin no joshu 支配人の助手
associate company keiretsu-gaisha 系列会社
association:
  trade association dōgyō-kumiai 同業組合
assurance:
  quality assurance hinshitsu-hoshō 品質保証
at par gakumen de 額面で
attitude:
  user attitude shōhisha no taido 消費者の態度
attitude survey taido-chōsa 態度調査
audio-visual aids shichōkaku-kizai 視聴覚機材
audit *v.* kansa-suru 監査する
audit kaikei-kansa 会計監査
  efficiency audit kōritsu-kansa 効率監査
  internal audit naibu-kansa 内部監査
  management audit keiei-kansa 経営監査
  manpower audit jin'in-hyō 人員表
  operations audit gyōmu-kansa 業務監査
  security audit anzen-hogo-kansa 安全保護監査

staff audit shokuin-kansa 職員監査
auditing:
balance sheet auditing taishaku-taishōhyō-kansa 貸借対照表監査
auditor kansayaku 監査役
authorized capital juken-shihon 授権資本
authority:
contraction of authority kenryoku no seigen 権力の制限
line authority rain-kengen ライン権限
authority structure kenryoku-kōzō 権力構造
automate *v.* jidōka-suru 自動化する
automation:
office automation jimu-jidōka 事務自動化
office automation design jimusho-jidōka no sekkei 事務所自動化の設計
average:
weighted average kajū-heikin 加重平均
average revenue heikin-shūnyū 平均収入
average yield heikin-rimawari 平均利回り
awareness:
market awareness shijō-ishiki 市場意識
awareness level ninshiki-suijun 認識水準

B

back-to-back loan sōsai-rōn 相殺ローン
back-up facility hojo-shisetsu 補助施設
backlog juchūzan 受注残
bad-debt losses kashi-daore-sonshitsu 貸し倒れ損失
bad debts furyō-saiken 不良債権
bad times fukeiki 不景気
balance sheet taishaku-taishōhyō 貸借対照表
balance sheet auditing taishaku-taishōhyō-kansa 貸借対照表監査
balanced portfolio kinkō no yoi shisan-naiyō 均衡のよい資産内容
ball game:
different ball game mattaku betsu no hanashi まったく別の話
bank:
commercial bank shōgyō-ginkō 商業銀行
computer bank konpyūta-banku コンピュータバンク
data bank dētā-banku データーバンク
investment bank tōshi-ginkō 投資銀行
merchant bank shōgyō-ginkō 商業銀行
safety bank anzen-kinko 安全金庫
bank rate ginkō-kinri 銀行金利
bar chart bōsen-zuhyō 棒線図表
bargaining:
collective bargaining dantai-kōshō 団体交渉
collective bargaining agreement dantai-rōdō-kyōyaku 団体労働協約
plant bargaining kōjō-reberu no kōshō 工場レベルの交渉
productivity bargaining seisansei-kōshō 生産性交渉
barrier:
non-tariff barrier (NTB) hikanzei-shōheki 非関税障壁
trade barrier bōeki-shōheki 貿易障壁
barter trade bātā-bōeki バーター貿易
base:
data base dētā-bēsu データーベース
base rate kihon-ryōkin 基本料金
base year kijun-nenji 基準年次
batch:
economic batch quantity keizai-batchi-sūryō 経済バッチ数量
batch control shūdan-kanri 集団管理
batch processing ikkatsu-shori 一括処理
batch production batchi-seisan バッチ生産
BCG (Boston Consulting Group) analysis bosuton-konsarutingu-gurūpu no bunseki ボストンコンサルティンググループの分析

bear yowakisuji 弱気筋
bear market yowaki-sōba 弱気相場
behaviour:
buying behaviour kōbai-kōdō 購買行動
consumer behaviour shōhisha-kōdō 消費者行動
behavioural science kōdō-kagaku 行動科学
below par gakumen-ika 額面以下
benchmark sokutei-kijun 測定基準
benefit:
cost-benefit analysis (CBA) hiyō-kōka-bunseki 費用効果分析
benefits:
fringe benefits chingin-igai no kyūfu 賃金以外の給付
bid:
leveraged bid rebarejjido-biddo レバレッジドビッド
pre-emptive bid shinkabu-hikiuke-nyūsatsu 新株引受入札
take-over bid (TOB) kabushiki no kōkai-kaitsuke 株式の公開買い付け
bill of credit shin'yō-jō 信用状
bit (binary digit) nishinhō-sūji 二進法数字
blackleg suto-yaburi スト破り
blue-chip yūryō-kabu 優良株
blue-chip stock negasa-kabu 値がさ株
blue-collar worker rōdōsha 労働者
blueprint sekkeizu 設計図
blue-sky (research) utagawashii kakaku (no chōsa) 疑わしい価格（の調査）
board:
executive board jōmukai 常務会
board control kanri-iinkai 管理委員会
board meeting torishimariyaku-kai 取締役会
board of directors jūyakukai 重役会
boardroom kaigishitsu 会議室
body language bodī-rangēji ボディーランゲージ
bond saiken 債券
junk bond janku-bondo ジャンクボンド
bonus shōyo 賞与
group bonus dantai-shōyo 団体賞与
premium bonus warimashi-shōyo 割増賞与
bonus scheme shōyo-seido 賞与制度
book value bojō-kakaku 簿上価格
boom kyūtō 急騰
booster training sai-kunren 再訓練
borrowing facility chintai-shisetsu 賃貸施設
Boston Box analysis bosuton-bokkusu-bunseki ボストンボックス分析
bottleneck shōgai 障害
bottom line saishū-kekka 最終結果
bottom out *v.* mukō ni suru 無効にする
bottom-up shita kara no iken-gushin 下からの意見具申
bottom-up strategy genba-

iken-saiyō-senryaku 現場意見採用戦略
brains trust senmonka-komon-dan 専門家顧問団
brainstorming burein-sutōmingu ブレインストーミング
branch office shisha 支社
brand burando ブランド
brand acceptance burando ni taisuru ninki ブランドに対する人気
brand awareness burando-ishiki ブランド意識
brand image burando-imēji ブランドイメージ
brand loyalty burando ni taisuru kodawari ブランドに対するこだわり
brand manager burando-manējā ブランドマネージャー
brand portfolio burando-pōtoforio ブランドポートフォリオ
brand positioning burando ni taisuru taido ブランドに対する態度
brand recognition burando-ninshiki ブランド認識
brand strategy burando-senryaku ブランド戦略
brand stretching shōhyō no yūkō-han'i 商標の有効範囲
break:
comfort break ian-kyūka 慰安休暇
stretch break kinchō o yawarageru kyūka 緊張をやわらげる休暇
breakdown:
operations breakdown sagyō-naiyō 作業内容
break even *v.* kinkō ni naru 均衡になる
break-even analysis son'eki-bunkiten-bunseki 損益分岐点分析
break-even point son'eki-bunkiten 損益分岐点
break-even quantity son'eki-bunki-ryō 損益分岐量
break-even sales son'eki-nashi no hanbai 損益なしの販売
breakthrough toppa 突破
break-up value seisan-kachi 生産価値
brief *v.* kanmei ni setsumei-suru 簡明に説明する
briefing gaiyō-setsumei 概要説明
broker nakagainin, burōkā 仲買人、ブローカー
software broker sofutouea-hanbai-gyōsha ソフトウエア販売業者
brokerage shūsen-ryō 周旋料
brokerage fees nakagai-tesū-ryō 仲買手数料
brown goods daidokoro-yōhin-igai no denki-seihin 台所用品以外の電器製品
budget *v.* yosan o kumu 予算を組む
budget yosan 予算
advertising budget kōkoku-yosan 広告予算
capital budget shihon-shishutsu-yosan 資本支出予算
cash budget genkin-shūshi-yosan 現金収支予算
flexible budget danryokusei-yosan 弾力性予算

investment budget tōshi-yosan 投資予算
marketing budget mākettingu-yosan マーケッティング予算
sales budget hanbai-yosoku 販売予測
zero-base budget yūsen-jun'i o bappontekini minaoshite sakuseishita yosan 優先順位を抜本的に見直して作成した予算
budget allotment yosan-haibun 予算配分
budget appropriation yosan-wariate 予算割当
budget constraint yosanteki-seiyaku 予算的制約
budget forecast yosan-mitōshi 予算見通し
budget forecasting yosan-yosoku 予算予測
budgetary control yosan-kanri 予算管理
budgeting yosan-hensei 予算編成
capital budgeting shihon-shishutsu-yosan 資本支出予算
cash budgeting genkin-shishutsu-yosan 現金支出予算
output budgeting sanshutsu-yosan 産出予算
performance budgeting gyōmu-yosan (-sakusei) 業務予算（作成）
budgeting control yosan-hensei-kanri 予算編成管理
buffer stock kanshō-zaiko 緩衝材庫
bug konpyūta no ayamari コンピュータの誤り
building:
team-building chīmu-zukuri チーム作り
built-in kumikomi 組み込み
built-in obsolescence kōzōteki-chinpuka 構造的陳腐化
bull tsuyokisuji 強気筋
bull market kaikata-shijō 買い方市場
bulletin board kōhō-keijiban 公報掲示板
bundling bandoru-sōsa バンドル操作
bureau:
employment bureau koyō-kyoku 雇用局
business centric bijinesu-chūshin (-no) ビジネス中心（の）
business corporation eiri-hōjin 営利法人
business cycle keiki-junkan 景気循環
business economist keiei-gakusha 経営学者
business forecasting keiki-yosoku 景気予測
business game bijinesu-gēmu ビジネスゲーム
business management kigyō-keiei 企業経営
business outlook bijinesu-mitōshi ビジネス見通し
business policy keiei-hōshin 経営方針
business portfolio bijinesu-pōtoforio ビジネスポートフォリオ
business relations torihiki-kankei 取引関係
business strategy keiei-senryaku 経営戦略

business stream keiki-dōkō 景気動向
business system bijinesu-soshiki ビジネス組織
business unit jigyōtai 事業体
strategic business unit senryakuteki-bijinesu-tan'i 戦略的ビジネス単位
buy in *v.* shiireru 仕入れる
buy out *v.* kaitoru 買い取る
buyer:
chief buyer kōbai-tantōsha 購買担当者
potential buyer senzaiteki-kaite 潜材的買い手
buyers' market kaite-shijō 買い手市場
buying:
impulse buying shōdō-gai 衝動買い
buying behaviour kōbai-kōdō 購買行動
buyout: kaiire 買い入れ
employee buyout jūgyōin no jisha-kaitori 従業員の自社買取
leveraged buyout (LBO) rebarejjido-baiauto レバレッジドバイアウト
management buyout (MBO) keieisha no jisha-kaitori 経営者の自社買取
worker buyout shain no jisha-kaitori 社員の自社買取
buzz-word bazu-wādo バズワード（ある分野で使われる特殊用語）
bypass *v.* ukai-suru 迂回する
by-product fukusanbutsu 副産物
byte go no ichikubun 語の一区分

C

CAD (computer-aided design) konpyūta ni yoru dezain コンピュータによるデザイン
CAL (computer-aided learning) konpyūta ni yoru gakushū コンピュータによる学習
CAM (computer-aided manufacturing) konpyūta ni yoru seizō コンピュータによる製造
campaign:
advertising campaign senden-katsudō, kyanpēn 宣伝活動，キャンペーン
productivity campaign seisansei-kōjō-undō 生産性向上運動
canvass *v.* chūmon-tori ni mawaru, kanyū-suru 注文取りに回る，勧誘する
capability nōryoku 能力
capacity:
excess capacity kajō-setsubi 過剰設備
full capacity zennōryoku 全能力
idle capacity yūkyū-shisetsu 遊休施設
manufacturing capacity seisan-nōryoku 生産能力
plant capacity shisetsu-nōryoku 施設能力
spare capacity yobi-seisan-nōryoku 予備生産能力
capacity utilization shisetsu-riyō-do 施設利用度
capex (capital expenditure) shihon-shishutsu 資本支出
capital:
authorized capital juken-shihon 授権資本
circulating capital ryūdō-shihon 流動資本
issued capital hakkō-zumi-kabushiki shihonkin 発行済み株式資本金
loan capital kashitsuke-shihon 貸付資本
return on capital shihon-kōritsu 資本効率
return on capital employed (ROCE) shiyō-shihon-kōritsu 使用資本効率
risk capital kiken-shihon 危険資本
share capital kabushiki-shihon 株式資本
venture capital benchā-shihon ベンチャー資本
working capital unten-shikin 運転資金
capital adequacy shihon-datōsei 資本妥当性
capital allowance shihon-hikiatekin 資本引当金
capital appreciation shihon-shobun 資本処分
capital assets kotei-shisan 固定資産
capital budget shihon-shishutsu-yosan 資本支出予算
capital budgeting shihon-shishutsu-yosan 資本支出予算
capital commitment shihon-itaku 資本委託
capital employed shiyō-shihongaku 使用資本額
capital expenditure shihon-shishutsu 資本支出

capital expenditure appraisal shihon-shishutsu-satei 資本支出査定
capital formation shihon-keisei 資本形成
capital gain shihonteki-rijun 資本的利潤
capital goods shihonzai 資本財
capital-intensive shihon-shūyakuteki 資本集約的
capital loss shihonteki-sonshitsu 資本的損失
capital-output ratio shihon-keisū 資本係数
capital project evaluation shihon-keikaku-hyōka 資本計画評価
capital raising shihon-chōtatsu 資本調達
capital structure shihon-kōsei 資本構成
capitalist:
venture capitalist kiken-futan-shihonka 危険負担資本家
capitalization shihon-kumiire 資本組み入れ
capitalize *v.* shihon ni kumi-ireru 資本に組み入れる
car phone jidōsha-denwa 自動車電話
care:
customer care kokyaku ni taisuru hairyo 顧客に対する配慮
career planning keireki-keikaku 経歴計画
cartel karuteru カルテル
case study kēsu-sutadi ケーススタディ
cash:
petty cash koguchi-genkin 小口現金
cash budget genkin-shūshi-yosan 現金収支予算
cash budgeting genkin-shūshi-yosan-hensei 現金収支予算編成
cash deal genkin-torihiki 現金取引
cash flow genkin-ryūdō, shikin-guri 現金流動, 資金操り
discounted cash flow (DCF) genkin-shūshi-waribiki 現金収支割引
incremental cash flow zōbun-genkin-furō 増分現金フロー
negative cash flow fusai no ryūdō 負債の流動
cash management genkin-kanri 現金管理
cash-poor genkinbusoku-jōtai 現金不足状態
cash ratio genkin-hiritsu 現金比率
cash-rich yutaka na temoto-ryūdō-sei 豊かな手元流動性
cash-strapped genkin-hippaku 現金逼迫
CAT (computer-assisted teaching) konpyūta ni yoru kyōiku コンピュータによる教育
CBA (cost-benefit analysis) hiyō-kōka-bunseki 費用効果分析
CBT (computer-based training) konpyūta ni motozuku kunren コンピュータに基づく訓練
ceiling:
wage ceiling kyūryō no jōgen

給料の上限
cellphone keitai-denwa 携帯電話
central processing unit (CPU) chūō-enzan-shori-sōchi 中央演算処理装置
centralization shūchūka 集中化
centralize *v.* shūchūka-suru 集中化する
centre:
assessment centre zeigaku-satei-jimusho 税額査定事務所
computer centre konpyūta-sentā コンピュータセンター
cost centre genka-bumon 原価部門
profit centre rieki-tan'i-bumon 利益単位部門
profit centre accounting rieki-tan'i-bumon-kaikei 利益単位部門会計
centric:
business centric bijinesu-chūshin (-no) ビジネス中心（の）
chain:
value chain kachi-taikei 価値体系
chain of command meirei-keitō 命令系統
chain of distribution ryūtsū-keitō 流通系統
chairman kaichō 会長
deputy chairman kaichō-dairi 会長代理
vice-chairman fuku-kaichō 副会長
challenge:
job challenge shigoto e no chōsen 仕事への挑戦
change management henkō-kanri 変更管理
channel:
distribution channel ryūtsū-keiro 流通経路
channel captain channeru-kantoku チャンネル監督
channels of communication komyunikēshon-channeru コミュニケーションチャンネル
channels of distribution ryū-tsū-channeru 流通チャンネル
chart:
activity chart gyōmuhyō 業務表
bar chart bōsen-zuhyō 棒線図表
flow chart nagarezu 流れ図
flow process chart nagare-sagyō-kōteizu 流れ作業工程図
management chart kanri-zuhyō 管理図表
milestone chart shuyō-kanriten-ichiranhyō 主要管理点一覧表
organization chart soshikizu 組織図
pie chart nikkahyō 日課表
Z chart zetto-zuhyō ゼット図表
chief accountant kaikei-sekininsha 会計責任者
chief buyer kōnyū-sekininsha 購入責任者
chief executive saikō-keiei-sekininsha 最高経営責任者
Chinese wall sōgo-rikai o samatageru mono 相互理解を妨げるもの
chip chippu チップ
computer memory chip kioku-chippu 記憶チップ
chunk a project *v.* keikaku o hōki-suru 計画を放棄する

chunk down *v.* bunkai-suru 分解する
CIM (computer-integrated manufacturing) konpyūta ni yoru tōgō-seisan コンピュータによる統合生産
circle:
quality circle hinshitsu-kanri-shō-gurūpu 品質管理小グループ
circulating capital ryūdō-shihon 流動資本
classification:
job classification shokkai 職階
clause:
no-strike clause sutoraiki-kinshi-jōkō ストライキ禁止条項
clearing house seisanjo 精算所
clerical work measurement (CWM) jimu-jikan-sokutei 事務時間測定
clerical worker jimu-shokuin 事務職員
climate:
economic climate keizai-kishō 経済気象
closed loop tojita rūpu 閉じたループ
closed shop kurōzudo-shoppu クローズドショップ
closing-down costs heiten-hiyō 閉店費用
co-determination kyōdō-kettei 共同決定
COINS (computerized information system) konpyūta-riyō-jōhō-shisutemu コンピュータ利用情報システム
collaborative kyōryokuteki 協力的
collateral tanpo (-shōken) 担保（証券）
collateral security tanpo-shōken 担保証券
collective bargaining dantai-kōshō 団体交渉
collective bargaining agreement dantai-rōdō-kyōyaku 団体労働協約
collusion dangō 談合
comfort break ian-kyūka 慰安休暇
command:
chain of command meirei-keitō 命令系統
line of command meirei-keitō 命令系統
commercial bank shōgyō-ginkō 商業銀行
commitment:
capital commitment shihon-itaku 資本委託
staff commitment shokuin-shokumu 職員職務
committee:
works committee kōjō-iinkai 工場委員会
commoditize *v.* shōhinka-suru 商品化する
commodity shōhin 商品
low-cost commodity tei-kakaku-shōhin 低価格商品
primary commodity ichiji-sanpin 一次産品
commodity exchange shōhin-torihiki 商品取引
commodity market shōhin-shijō 商品市場
common currency kyōtsū-tsūka 共通通貨

common language kyōtsūgo 共通語
Common Market yōroppa-keizai-kyōdōtai ヨーロッパ経済共同体
communication:
channels of communication tsūshin-channeru 通信チャンネル
communications network tsūshin-mō 通信網
communications theory tsūshin-riron 通信理論
company:
affiliate company kogaisha 子会社
associate company mochikabu-gaisha 持ち株会社
joint venture company gōben-gaisha 合弁会社
parent company oya-gaisha 親会社
publicly listed company jōjō-kigyō 上場企業
quoted company jōjō-kigyō 上場企業
subsidiary company shitauke-gaisha 下請け会社
system-managed company shisutemu-kanri-kigyō システム管理企業
unlisted company hi-jōjō-kigyō 非上場企業
company goal kigyō-mokuhyō 企業目標
company logo kigyō-māku 企業マーク
company objective kigyō-mokuteki 企業目的
company philosophy kigyō-tetsugaku 企業哲学
company planning kigyō-keikaku 企業計画
company policy kaisha no hōshin 会社の方針
company profit kigyō-shūeki 企業収益
company reconstruction kigyō-saiken 企業再建
comparison:
inter-firm comparison keiei-hikaku 経営比較
compartmentalize *v.* chiiki-bunkatsuka-suru 地域分割化する
compatibility gokansei 互換性
compatible gokansei ga aru 互換性がある
compensation:
executive compensation yakuin-hōshū 役員報酬
job compensation shokumu-hōshū 職務報酬
competency kōdō-nōryoku 行動能力
competition:
fair competition kōsei na kyōsō 公正な競争
unfair competition fukōsei na kyōsō 不公正な競争
competitive kyōsōteki 競争的
competitive advantage kyōsōjō no yūi 競争上の優位
competitive edge kyōsōteki-yūi 競争的優位
competitive position kyōsōteki-shisei 競争的姿勢
competitive price kyōsō-kakaku 競争価格
competitive stimulus kyōsōteki-shigeki 競争的刺激
competitive strategy kyōsō-senryaku 競争戦略
competitive tactics

kyōsō-senjutsu 競争戦術
competitive tendering kyōsō-nyūsatsu 競争入札
competitive thrust kyōsōteki-kōgeki 競争的攻撃
competitiveness jiyū-kyōsō 自由競争
competitor analysis kyōsō-kankei-bunseki 競争関係分析
complex:
production complex seisan-fukugōtai 生産複合体
comptroller kaikei-kansakan 会計監査官
computer konpyūta コンピュータ
analog computer anarogu-konpyūta アナログコンピュータ
desktop computer takujō-gata-konpyūta 卓上型コンピュータ
digital computer dejitaru-konpyūta デジタルコンピュータ
laptop computer rappu-toppu-gata-konpyūta ラップトップ型コンピュータ
personal computer (PC) paso-kon パソコン
computer-aided design (CAD) konpyūta-riyō-sekkei コンピュータ利用設計
computer-aided learning (CAL) konpyūta-riyō-gakushū コンピュータ利用学習
computer-aided manufacturing (CAM) konpyūta-riyō-seizō コンピュータ利用製造
computer-assisted teaching (CAT) konpyūta-riyō-kyōiku コンピュータ利用教育
computer bank konpyūta-banku コンピュータバンク
computer-based training (CBT) konpyūta ni motozuku kunren コンピュータに基づく訓練
computer centre konpyūta-sentā コンピュータセンター
computer consultant konpyūta-konsarutanto コンピュータコンサルタント
computer expert konpyūta-jukurensha コンピュータ熟練者
computer input nyūryoku-sōchi 入力装置
computer language konpyūta-gengo コンピュータ言語
computer literate konpyūta-jōhōriron コンピュータ情報理論
computer memory konpyūta-kioku (-sōchi) コンピュータ記憶（装置）
computer memory chip kioku-chippu 記憶チップ
computer output shutsuryoku-sōchi 出力装置
computer program konpyūta-puroguramu コンピュータプログラム
computer programmer konpyūta-puroguramā コンピュータプログラマー
computer programming konpyūta-puroguramingu コンピュータプログラミング
computer services konpyūta-keisan, konpyūta-sābisu コンピュータ計算，コンピュータサービス
computer services bureau konpyūta-keisan-sentā コンピュータ計算センター

computer simulation konpyūta-shimyurēshon コンピュータシミュレーション
computer storage konpyūta-kioku-sōchi コンピュータ記憶装置
computer terminal konpyūta-tanmatsuki コンピュータ端末機
computer virus konpyūta-uirusu コンピュータウイルス
computerize konpyūtaka-suru コンピュータ化する
computerized information system (COINS) konpyūta-riyō-jōhō-shisutemu コンピュータ利用情報システム
conception:
product conception seihin-gainen 製品概念
conciliate *v.* wakai-suru 和解する
conciliation chōtei 調停
conditions of employment koyō-jōken 雇用条件
confidentiality kimitsusei 機密性
conglomerate konguromaritto コングロマリット
consciousness:
cost consciousness genka-ishiki 原価意識
consensus gōi 合意
consolidated accounts renketsu-kessan 連結決算
consolidation renketsu 連結
consortium gōben-gaisha 合弁会社
constraint:
budget constraint yosan-teki-seiyaku 予算的制約
consult *v.* sōdan-suru 相談する
consultancy konsarutanto-gyō コンサルタント業
management consultancy keiei-konsarutanto-gyō 経営コンサルタント業
consultant konsarutanto コンサルタント
computer consultant konpyūta-konsarutanto コンピュータコンサルタント
management consultant keiei-konsarutanto 経営コンサルタント
consultation:
joint consultation rōshi-kyōgi 労使協議
consultative komon 顧問
consumables shōmōhin 消耗品
consumer:
fast-moving consumer goods (FMCG) kō-kaiten-shōhi-busshi 高回転消費物資
consumer acceptance tokuisaki-hikiuke-tegata 得意先引受手形
consumer behaviour shōhisha-kōdō 消費者行動
consumer convergence shōhisha-shūgō 消費者集合
consumer durables taikyū-shōhizai 耐久消費財
consumer goods shōhizai, shōhi-busshi 消費財、消費物資
consumer orientation kokyaku-shikō 顧客志向
consumer price index shōhisha-bukka-shisū 消費者物価指数
consumer protection shōhisha-hogo 消費者保護
consumer research shōhisha-

chōsa 消費者調査
consumer resistance kōbai-kyohi 購買拒否
consumer-responsive shōhisha-han'nō 消費者反応
consumer satisfaction shōhisha-manzoku 消費者満足
consumerism shōhisha-katsudō 消費者活動
consumers' panel shōhisha-meibo 消費者名簿
container kontena コンテナ
containerization kontenaka コンテナ化
content:
work content sagyō-naiyō 作業内容
contingencies gūhatsusei 偶発性
contingency gūhatsu 偶発
contingency planning saigai-taisaku 災害対策
contingency reserve gūhatsu-sonshitsu-hikiatekin 偶発損失引当金
contingency theory gūhatsu-riron 偶発理論
continuous-flow production renzoku-nagare-sagyō-seisan 連続流れ作業生産
continuous stocktaking renzoku-zaikohin-shirabe 連続在庫品調べ
contract:
management contract keiei-keiyaku 経営契約
work by contract keiyaku no rikō 契約の履行
contract hire keiyaku-koyō 契約雇用
contract out *v.* gaibu ni hatchū-suru 外部に発注する
contracting out gaibu-hatchū 外部発注
contraction of authority ken-gen no shukushō 権限の縮小
contribution analysis kōkendo-bunseki 貢献度分析
control kanri 管理
adaptive control jun'nō-seigyo 順応制御
administrative control procedure un'ei-kanri-hōshiki 運営管理方式
batch control batchi-seigyo バッチ制御
board control torishimari-yakukai ni yoru kanri 取締役会による管理
budgetary control yosan-kanri 予算管理
cost control genka-kanri 原価管理
financial control zaimu-kanri 財務管理
inventory control zaiko-kanri 在庫管理
managerial control kanriteki-tōsei 管理的統制
manufacturing control seizō-kanri 製造管理
numerical control sūchi-seigyo 数値制御
process control kōtei-kanri 工程管理
production control seisan-kanri 生産管理
production planning and control seisan-keikaku-kanri 生産計画管理
progress control shindo-kanri (seisan-kōtei no) 進度管理（生産工程の）
quality control (QC)

hinshitsu-kanri 品質管理
span of control kanri-genkai 管理限界
statistical control tōkeiteki-kanri 統計的管理
stock control zaiko-kanri 在庫管理
control information seigyo-jōhō 制御情報
controller kanrishoku 管理職
controlling interest shihaiteki-riken 支配的利権
convenience goods jōyōhin 常用品
convergence:
consumer convergence shōhisha no shūchūsei 消費者の集中性
coordination chōsei-katsudō 調整活動
core strategy chūkaku-senryaku 中核戦略
corner kaishime 買い占め
corner *v.* kaishimeru 買い占める
corner the market *v.* shijō o kaishimeru 市場を買い占める
corporate advertising kigyō-kōkoku 企業広告
corporate culture kigyō-bunka 企業文化
corporate growth kigyō-seichō 企業成長
corporate image kigyō-imēji 企業イメージ
corporate model zensha-moderu 全社モデル
corporate planning kigyō-keikaku 企業計画
corporate raider nottoriya 乗っ取り屋
corporate strategy kigyō-senryaku 企業戦略
corporate structure kigyō-kōzō 企業構造
corporation:
business corporation jigyō-gaisha 事業会社
corporation tax hōjinzei 法人税
corporatism kyōdō-kumiai-shugi 協同組合主義
correlate *v.* kanren-saseru 関連させる
correlation sōkan-kankei 相関関係
cost accounting genka-kaikei 原価会計
cost analysis genka-bunseki 原価分析
cost awareness genka-ishiki 原価意識
cost-benefit analysis (CBA) hiyō-ben'eki-bunseki 費用便益分析
cost centre genka-chūshinten 原価中心点
cost consciousness genka-ishiki 原価意識
cost control genka-kanri 原価管理
cost-effective hiyō-tai-kōka 費用対効果
cost-effectiveness hiyō-kōka 費用効果
cost-efficient hiyō-kōritsu 費用効率
cost factor hiyō-yōin 費用要因
cost of living seikeihi 生計費
cost of production seisan-genka 生産原価
cost-push inflation hiyō-appaku-infure 費用圧迫インフレ

cost reduction genka-hikisage 原価引き下げ
cost-sensitive hiyō-binkansei 費用敏感性
cost standard genka-kijun 原価基準
cost structure genka-kōsei 原価構成
cost variance genka-sagaku 原価差額
cost-volume-profit analysis son'eki-bunseki 損益分析
costing genka-keisan 原価計算
absorption costing zentai-genka-keisan 全体原価計算
direct costing chokusetsu-genka (keisan) 直接原価（計算）
functional costing bumon-betsu-genka-keisan 部門別原価計算
marginal costing genkai-genka-keisan 限界原価計算
product costing kobetsu-genka-keisan 個別原価計算
standard costing hyōjun-genka-keisan 標準原価計算
variable costing hendō-genka-keisan 変動原価計算
costs:
allocation of costs genka no haibun 原価の配分
average costs heikin-genka 平均原価
closing-down costs heiten-hiyō 閉店費用
direct costs chokusetsu-genka 直接原価
distribution costs ryūtsū-keihi 流通経費
estimating systems costs mitsumori-genka-sei 見積原価制
fixed costs koteihi 固定費
indirect costs kansetsu-hiyō 間接費用
labour costs rōmuhi 労務費
managed costs kanri-kanō-hiyō 管理可能費用
marginal costs genkai-hiyō 限界費用
opportunity costs kikai-hiyō 機会費用
replacement costs saishutoku-genka 再取得原価
semi-variable costs jun-hendōhi 準変動費
set-up costs setchi-hiyō 設置費用
standard costs hyōjun-hiyō 標準費用
start-up costs setsuritsu-hiyō 設立費用
unit labour costs bumon-betsu-rōmuhi 部門別労務費
variable costs kahenhi 可変費
council:
works council rōshi-kyōgikai 労使協議会
counselling:
employee counselling jūgyōin-kaunseringu 従業員カウンセリング
countertrade mikaeri-torihiki 見返り取引
cover ratio hoshōkin-ritsu 保証金率
coverage:
sales coverage sērusu-kabarejji セールスカバレッジ
CPA (critical path analysis)

kuritikaru-pasu-bunseki クリティカルパス分析
CPI (consumer price index) shōhisha-bukka-shisū 消費者物価指数
CPM (critical path method) kuritikaru-pasu-bunsekihō クリティカルパス分析法
CPU (central processing unit) chūō-enzan-shori-sōchi 中央演算処理装置
crash kyōkō 恐慌
crash (a program) *v.* (keikaku o) tsubusu （計画を）潰す
creative accounting sōzō-kanjō 創造勘定
creative marketing sōzōteki-shijō 創造的市場
creative thinking sōzōteki-shikō 創造的思考
credit:
 revolving credit kaiten-shin'yō-kanjō 回転信用勘定
credit control shin'yō-kanri 信用管理
credit management shin'yō-kanri 信用管理
credit rating shin'yō-kakuzuke 信用格付け
credit squeeze kin'yū-hikishime 金融引き締め
crisis management kiki-kanri 危機管理
criteria:
 investment criteria tōshi-kijun 投資基準
critical mass genkai-ryō 限界量
critical path analysis (CPA) saichō-keiro-bunseki 最長経路分析
critical path method kuritikaru-pasu-messodo クリティカル・パス・メソッド
cross-licensing sōgo-tokkyo-shiyōken 相互特許使用権
culture bunka 文化
 corporate culture kigyō-bunka 企業文化
 organization culture soshiki-bunka 組織文化
currency:
 common currency kyōtsū-tsūka 共通通貨
 parallel currency taiō-tsūka 対応通貨
 single currency tan'itsu-tsūka 単一通貨
current assets ryūdō-shisan 流動資産
 net current assets jun-ryūdō-shisan 準流動資産
current expenditure keijōhi 経常費
current liabilities ryūdō-fusai 流動負債
current ratio ryūdō-hiritsu 流動比率
cursor ichi-hyōji-kikō 位置表示機構
curve:
 learning curve shūjuku-kyokusen 習熟曲線
 salary progression curve kyūyo-jōshō-kyokusen 給与上昇曲線
custom and practice kankō 慣行
custom-made chūmon-seisan 注文生産
customer care kokyaku ni tai-suru hairyo 顧客に対する配慮
customer orientation kokyaku-shidō 顧客指導

customer profit kokyaku-rijun 顧客利潤

customer service kokyaku-hōshi 顧客奉仕

customized chūmon-seisan-shita 注文生産した

cut one's losses *v.* sonshitsu o sakugen-suru 損失を削減する

cut prices *v.* nebiki-suru 値引きする

cut-off point uchikiri-gendo 打ち切り限度

cutting:

price cutting nebiki 値引き

cutting edge setsudan-ba 切断刃

CWM (clerical work measurement) jimu-jikan-sokutei 事務時間測定

cycle:

business cycle keiki-junkan 景気循環

life cycle (of a product) jumyō (seihin no) 寿命（製品の）

work cycle sagyō-saikuru 作業サイクル

D

daisy wheel hinagiku-gata-sharin 雛菊型車輪
damage limitation exercise songai-gentei-renshū 損害限定練習
data acquisition dētā-shūshū データー収集
data bank dētā-banku データーバンク
data base dētā-bēsu データーベース
data costing dētā-genka-keisan データー原価計算
data expenses dētā-hiyō データー費用
data flow chart dētā nagare-zu データー流れ図
data mail dētā-tsūshin データー通信
data protection dētā-hogo データー保護
data retrieval dētā-kensaku データー検索
data selling dētā-hanbai データー販売
date:
due date shiharai-kijitsu 支払期日
expected date yotei-kijitsu 予定期日
latest date saishin-kijitsu 最新期日
sell-by date baikyaku-kijitsu 売却期日
use-by date shiyō-kikan 使用期間
day shift ichinichi-kōtai-sei 一日交代制
DCF (discounted cash flow) genkin-shūshi-waribiki 現金収支割引
deadline shimekiri-bi 締め切り日
deal torihiki 取引
cash deal genkin-torihiki 現金取引
reach a deal v. keiyaku ni tassuru 契約に達する
dealer dīrā ディーラー
dealing:
insider dealing insaidā-torihiki インサイダー取引
debottleneck v. airo o kaishō-suru 隘路を解消する
debrief v. jōhō o ukeru 情報を受ける
debriefing taiken no kikitori 体験の聞き取り
debt financing fusai ni yoru shikin-chōtatsu 負債による資金調達
debt-equity ratio fusai-tai-shihon-ritsu 負債対資本率
debts:
bad debts furyō-saiken 不良債権
decentralize v. bunsanka-suru 分散化する
decentralized management bunkenteki-keiei 分権的経営
declaration shinkoku 申告
deductible:
tax-deductible zeikin-kōjo 税金控除
deduction:
payroll deduction chingin-kōjo 賃金控除
deficit financing akaji-zaisei 赤字財政

deindustrialization kōgyōryoku no hakai 工業力の破壊
delegate *v.* daihyō-suru 代表する
delivery time nōki 納期
demand forecasting juyō-yosoku 需要予測
demand-pull inflation juyō-infure 需要インフレ
demanning jin'in-sakugen 人員削減
demerger kigyō no kaisan 企業の解散
demotivate *v.* dōki o ubau 動機を奪う
demotivation dōki-hakai 動機破壊
departmental manager bumon-kanrisha 部門管理者
deploy *v.* haichi-suru 配置する
depreciate *v.* genka-shōkyaku-suru 原価償却する
deputy managing director jōmu-torishimari-yaku-ho 常務取締役補
deregulate *v.* kisei o kanwa-suru 規制を緩和する
deregulation kisei-kanwa 規制緩和
descaling fuyōbutsu no jokyo 不要物の除去
design office sekkei jimusho 設計事務所
desktop takujōgata 卓上型
desktop computer takujōgata-konpyūta 卓上型コンピュータ
desktop publish *v.* denshi-shuppan-suru 電子出版する
desktop publishing denshi-shuppan 電子出版
developer kaihatsu-gyōsha 開発業者
development:
human resource development (HRD) jinteki-shigen-kaihatsu 人的資源開発
diagnostic routine shindan-rūchin 診断ルーチン
diagram:
flow diagram nagare-sagyōzu 流れ作業図
differential pricing sabetsu-teki-kakaku-seido 差別的価格制度
differentiate *v.* sabetsuka-suru 差別化する
product differentiate *v.* seihin o sabetsuka (-suru) 製品を差別化（する）
digital dejitaru デジタル
digitize *v.* keisūka-suru 計数化する
digitizing (comp) keisūka 計数化
dinkie tomobataraki de kodomo no nai fūfu 共働きで子供のない夫婦
direct hire chokusetsu-koyō 直接雇用
direct marketing chokusetsu-hanbai 直接販売
director yakuin 役員
deputy managing director jōmu-torishimariyaku-ho 常務取締役補
executive director senmu-torishimariyaku 専務取締役
financial director zaimu-sekininsha 財務責任者
managing director (MD) jōmu-torishimariyaku 常務取

締役
non-executive director hijōkin-torishimariyaku 非常勤取締役
outside director shagai-jūyaku 社外重役
directorate:
interlocking directorate kennin-jūyakukai 兼任重役会
directors:
board of directors torishimariyaku-kai 取締役会
disburse *v.* shiharau 支払う
disbursement genkin-shiharai 現金支払
discounted cash flow (DCF) genkin-shūshi-waribiki 現金収支割引
discretion:
time span of discretion jiyū-sairyō-jikantai 自由裁量時間帯
discriminate *v.* sabetsu-suru 差別する
discrimination sabetsu (-taigū) 差別（待遇）
positive discrimination sekkyokuteki-sabetsu 積極的差別
price discrimination kakaku-sabetsu 価格差別
diseconomy of scale kibo no fukeizaisei 規模の不経済性
disincentive keizai-seichō-sogai (-yōin) 経済成長阻害（要因）
disintegration hōkai 崩壊
disinvestment tōshi-busoku 投資不足
disk jiki-disuku 磁気ディスク
hard disk hādo-disuku ハードディスク
Winchester disk uinchesutā-disuku ウインチェスターディスク
disk drive disuku-doraibu ディスクドライブ
dismissal kaiko 解雇
constructive dismissal itsuwari-no-kaiko 偽りの解雇
summary dismissal sokketsu-kyoka 即決許可
unfair dismissal futō-kaiko 不当解雇
dispatching sagyō-haibun 作業配分
display unit (comp) eizō-hyōji-sōchi 映像表示装置
visual display unit (VDU) hyōji-sōchi 表示装置
disposable income kashobun-shotoku 可処分所得
disposition:
source and disposition of funds shikin-un'yōhyō 資金運用表
dispute:
industrial dispute rōdō-sōgi 労働争議
labour dispute rōshi-funsō 労使紛争
dissolution kaisan 解散
distance learning gakugai deno gakushū 学外での学習
distribution haibun 配分
chain of distribution ryūtsū-keitō 流通系統
channels of distribution ryūtsū-channeru 流通チャンネル
frequency distribution dosū-bunpu 度数分布
physical distribution management butteki-ryūtsū-

kanri 物的流通管理
distribution channel ryūtsū-keiro 流通経路
distribution costs ryūtsū-keihi 流通経費
distribution management ryūtsū-kanri 流通管理
distribution manager ryūtsū-sekininsha 流通責任者
distribution network ryūtsū-keiro 流通経路
distribution planning ryūtsū-keikaku 流通計画
distribution policy hanbai-hōshin 販売方針
diversification tayōka 多様化
product diversification seihin-tayōka 製品多様化
diversification strategy tayōka-senryaku 多様化戦略
diversify *v.* tayōka-suru 多様化する
divestment shoyūken-hakudatsu 所有権はく奪
dividend haitō 配当
dividend policy haitō-seisaku 配当政策
division:
operating division jigyō-bumon 事業部門
divisional management bumon-kanri 部門管理
doomwatcher unmei-kanshinin 運命監視人
double taxation relief nijū-kazei-menjo 二重課税免除
down-market kakō-sōba 下降相場
down the line zenmenteki na 全面的な
down time kyūshi-jikan 休止時間
downside warui-men 悪い面
downstream kawashimo (sangyō-no) 川下（産業の）
downswing kakō-kyokumen 下降局面
downturn kakō 下降
wage drift kōshō-chinginsa 交渉賃金差
drag:
fiscal drag zaiseiteki-shōgai 財政的障害
drip-feeding jojo ni hokyū-suru 徐々に補給する
drive:
advertising drive senden-katsudō 宣伝活動
disk drive disuku-doraibu ディスクドライブ
productivity drive seisan-sei-kōjō-undō 生産性向上運動
sales drive hanbai-sokushin 販売促進
dual sourcing nijū-kyōkyūgen 二重供給源
due date shiharai-kijitsu 支払期日
dummy activity giji-sagyō 疑似作業
dumping futō-renbai 不当廉売
durables taikyūzai 耐久財
consumer durables taikyū-shōhizai 耐久消費財
dynamic evaluation dōteki-hyōkahō 動的評価法
dynamic management model dōtaikeiei-moderu 動態経営モデル
dynamic programming dōteki-keikakuhō 動的計画法
dynamic ratio dōtai-hiritsu 動態比率
dynamics:

group dynamics shūdan-rikigaku 集団力学
industrial dynamics kigyō-dōtaigaku 企業動態学
market dynamics shijō-rikigaku 市場力学
product dynamics seisan-rikigaku 生産力学

dysfunction kinō-shōgai 機能障害

E

e-mail (electronic mail) denshi-yūbin 電子郵便
early retirement sōki-teinen 早期定年
earning power shūekiryoku 収益力
earnings:
price earnings ratio (P/E) kakaku-shūeki-ritsu 価格収益率
retained earnings shanai-ryūho-riekikin 社内留保利益金
earnings on assets shisan-shūeki 資産収益
earnings per share (EPS) hitokabu atari no shūeki 一株当たりの収益
earnings performance shūeki-gyōseki 収益業績
earnings yield shūeki-gaku 収益額
EC (European Community) ōshū-kyōdōtai 欧州共同体
econometric keiryō-keizai-gakuteki 計量経済学的
economic batch quantity keizai-batchi-sūryō 経済バッチ数量
economic condition keizai-kishō 経済気象
economic exposure keizai-kikendo 経済危険度
economic intelligence keizai-jōhō 経済情報
economic life kinōteki-taiyō-nensū 機能的耐用年数
economic manufacturing quantity saiteki-seisanryō 最適生産量
economic mission keizai-shisetsudan 経済使節団
economic order quantity saiteki-hatchūryō 最適発注量
economic research keizai-chōsa 経済調査
economic trend keizai-dōkō 経済動向
economist:
business economist keiei-gakusha 経営学者
economy:
motion economy dōsa-keizai 動作経済
economy of scale kibo no keizaisei 規模の経済性
ECU (European Currency Unit) ōshū-tsūka-tan'i 欧州通貨単位
ecu:
hard ecu kōkan-kanō no ōshū-tsūka 交換可能の欧州通貨
edge:
competitive edge kyōsō-teki-yūi 競争的優位
cutting edge kattingu-ejji カッティング・エッジ
leading edge rīdingu-ejji リーディング・エッジ
EDP (electronic data processing) denshishiki-dētā-shori 電子式データー処理
effective:
cost-effective hiyō-tai-kōka 費用対効果
effective management kōkateki na kanri 効果的な管理
effectiveness yūkōsei 有効性
advertising effectiveness

senden-kōka 宣伝効果
cost-effectiveness hiyō-kōka 費用効果
managerial effectiveness kanri-kōka 管理効果
organizational effectiveness soshikiteki-kōka 組織的効果
efficiency nōritsu 能率
efficiency audit kōritsu-kansa 効率監査
efficient yūkō 有効
cost-efficient hiyō no yūkō-sei 費用の有効性
effort:
sales expansion effort hanbai-kakuchō-doryoku 販売拡張努力
EFTOPS (electric funds transfer at point of sale) hanbai-chiten kara no denshi sō-kin 販売地点からの電子送金
elasticity danryokusei 弾力性
electronic data processing (EDP) denshishiki-dētā-shori 電子式データー処理
electronic mail (e-mail) denshi-yūbin 電子郵便
electronic office denshi-ka sareta jimusho 電子化された事務所
empirical bōkenteki 冒険的
employed:
capital employed shiyō-shihon-gaku 使用資本額
return on capital employed (ROCE) shiyō-shihon-kōritsu 使用資本効率
employee buyout jūgyōin no kaisha-kaitori 従業員の会社買い取り
employee counselling jūgyōin-kaunseringu 従業員カウンセリング
employee relations jūgyōin-kankei 従業員関係
employees:
direct hire employees chokusetsu-koyō-jūgyōin 直接雇用従業員
full-time employees jōkinsha 常勤者
employment koyō 雇用
conditions of employment koyō-jōken 雇用条件
full-time employment jōkin-koyō 常勤雇用
part-time employment hijōkin-koyō 非常勤雇用
employment bureau koyō-kyoku 雇用局
EMS (European Monetary System) ōshū-tsūka-seido 欧州通貨制度
EMU (European Monetary Union) ōshū-tsūka-dōmei 欧州通貨同盟
engineer gijutsusha 技術者
software engineer sofutouea-enjinia ソフトウエア・エンジニア
systems engineer shisu-temu-enjinia システム・エンジニア
engineering kōgaku-gijutsu 工学技術
design engineering sekkei-gijutsu 設計技術
human engineering ningen-kōgaku 人間工学
industrial engineering san-gyō-kōgaku 産業工学
methods engineering hōhō-kōgaku 方法工学

production engineering seisan-gijutsu 生産技術
simultaneous engineering dōji-shori-gijutsu 同時処理技術
systems engineering shisutemu-kōgaku システム工学
value engineering kachi-kōgaku 価値工学
engineering and design department gijutsu-sekkeibu 技術設計部
enlargement:
job enlargement shokumu-kakudai 職務拡大
enrichment:
job enrichment shokumu-kyōka 職務強化
enterprise kigyō 企業
private enterprise minkan-kigyō 民間企業
public enterprise kōei-kigyō 公営企業
enterprising kigyō-seishin ni tomu 企業精神に富む
entrepreneurial spirit kigyō-ka-seishin 企業家精神
environment kankyō 環境
environmental analysis kankyō-bunseki 環境分析
environmental forecasting kankyō-yosoku 環境予測
environmental scan kankyō-chōsa 環境調査
EPS (earnings per share) hitokabu atari no shūeki 一株当たりの収益
equal employment opportunity byōdō-koyō-kikai 平等雇用機会
equal pay dōitsu-chingin 同一賃金
equality byōdō 平等
equipment:
add-on equipment tsuika-shisetsu 追加施設
peripheral equipment shūhen-sōchi 周辺装置
process equipment layout seisan-kōtei-shisetsu no haichi 生産工程施設の配置
equipment leasing shisetsu-chintai(-keiyaku) 施設賃貸(契約)
equity kabunushi-ken 株主権
dilution of equity kabunushi-ken no kishaku 株主権の希釈
return on equity jun-shisan no shūeki-ritsu 純資産の収益率
equity market kabushiki-shijō 株式市場
ergonometrics sagyō-nōryoku 作業能力
ergonomics ningen-kōgaku 人間工学
ERM (Exchange Rate Mechanism) kawase-shijō 為替市場
escalation:
price escalation kakaku-jōshō 価格上昇
espionage:
industrial espionage sangyō-supai 産業スパイ
establishment setsuritsu 設立
estimate *v.* mitsumoru 見積る
estimate:
sales estimate uriage-mitsu-mori 売上見積
estimating systems costs mitsumori-genka-sei 見積原価制
Eurobond yūro-sai ユーロ債

Eurocurrency yūro-manē ユーロマネー
Eurodollar yūro-darā ユーロダラー
Euromarket ōshū-kyōdō-shijō 欧州共同市場
European Community (EC) ōshū-kyōdōtai 欧州共同体
European Currency Unit (ECU) ōshū-tsūka-tan'i 欧州通貨単位
European Monetary System (EMS) ōshū-tsūka-seido 欧州通貨制度
European Monetary Union (EMU) ōshū-tsūka-dōmei 欧州通貨同盟
evaluate *v.* hyōka-suru 評価する
evaluation:
 capital project evaluation tōshi-keikaku-hyōka 投資計画評価
 dynamic evaluation dōteki-hyōkahō 動的評価法
 job evaluation shokumu-satei 職務査定
 performance evaluation gyōseki-satei 業績査定
evolve strategy *v.* senryaku o tenkai-suru 戦略を展開する
***ex gratia* payment** mimaikin 見舞金
exception:
 management by exception reigai-kanri 例外管理
excess capacity kajō-setsubi 過剰設備
exchange rate:
 forward exchange rate sakimono-kawase-sōba 先物為替相場
Exchange Rate Mechanism (ERM) kawase-shijō 為替市場
execution:
 policy execution hōshin no jisshi 方針の実施
executive kanrishoku 管理職
 chief executive saikō-keiei-sekininsha 最高経営責任者
 line executive rain-bumon no sekininsha ライン部門の責任者
executive board jōmukai 常務会
executive competence kanri-nōryoku 管理能力
executive development keieisha-kaihatsu 経営者開発
executive director senmu-torishimariyaku 専務取締役
executive manpower strategy kanbu-jinzai-yōsei-senryaku 幹部人材養成戦略
executive search kanrishoku-saiyō (-jigyō) 管理職採用（事業）
executive staff strategy kanbu-shokuin-senryaku 幹部職員戦略
expand *v.* kakudai-suru 拡大する
expansion:
 sales expansion effort hanbai-kakuchō-doryoku 販売拡張努力
expansion strategy kakudai-senryaku 拡大戦略
expectations:
 job expectations shigoto no shōraisei 仕事の将来性
 sales expectations hanbai-yosō 販売予想
expected date yotei-kijitsu 予定期日
expenditure:
 capital expenditure

(capex) shihon-shishutsu 資本支出
current expenditure keijōhi 経常費
revenue expenditure (revex) sainyū-saishutsu 歳入歳出
expense account kōsaihi 交際費
expenses:
direct expenses chokusetsu-keihi 直接経費
indirect expenses kan-setsu-keihi 間接経費
petty expenses zappi 雑費
recovery of expenses keihi no kaishū 経費の回収
running expenses unten-keihi 運転経費
expert:
computer expert konpyūta-senmonka コンピュータ専門家
expert system senmonka-keiei-shisutemu 専門家経営システム
exploration:
market exploration shijō-chōsa 市場調査
explore *v.* tansaku-suru 探索する
exponential smoothing shisū-heikatsuhō 指数平滑法
exponential trend shisū-dōkō 指数動向
exposure kikendo 危険度
economic exposure keizai-teki-kikendo 経済的危険度
extension services kōhō-gyōmu-katsudō 公報業務活動
external relations taigai-kan-kei 対外関係
externalities shagai-kigyō 社外企業
externalize *v.* gaichū-suru 外注する

F

facsimile densō-shashin 伝送写真
factor yōso 要素
cost factor hiyō-yōin 費用要因
load factor fuka-ritsu 付加率
factoring saiken-kin'yū 債権金融
factoring urikakekin-saiken-kaitori 売掛金債権買取
factory overheads kōjō-kan-setsuhi 工場間接費
fair kōsei 公正
fair competition kōsei na kyōsō 公正な競争
fair return kōsei-hōshū 公正報酬
family tree keizu 系図
fast-moving consumer goods (FMCG) kōkaiten-shōhi-busshi 高回転消費物資
fast-track kōsoku-rosen 高速路線
fax *v.* fakkusu o okuru ファックスを送る
fax fakkusu ファックス
fax machine fakkusu-kiki ファックス機器
feasibility study junbi-chōsa 準備調査
feasible shōraisei 将来性
featherbedding mizumashi-koyō-yōkyū 水増し雇用要求
feedback fīdo-bakku フィードバック
fiddle *v.* gomakasu ごまかす
field research genchi-chōsa 現地調査
field testing shiunten 試運転
finance *v.* shikin o kyōkyū-suru 資金を供給する
financial administration zai-mu-kanri 財務管理
financial analysis zaimu-bunseki 財務分析
financial appraisal zaimu-satei 財務査定
financial control zaimu-kanri 財務管理
financial director zaimu-sekininsha 財務責任者
financial futures kin'yū-saki-mono-torihiki 金融先物取引
financial incentive zaiseiteki-shigeki 財政的刺激
financial management kin'yū-sōsa 金融操作
financial market kin'yū-shijō 金融市場
financial planning zaimu-keikaku 財務計画
financial position zaimu-jōtai 財務状態
financial ratio zaimu-hiritsu 財務比率
financial review zaimu-minaoshi 財務見直し
financial standard zaimu-kijun 財務基準
financial statement zaimu-shohyō 財務諸表
financial strategy zaimu-senryaku 財務戦略
financial year kaikei-nendo 会計年度
financing:
debt financing kokusai ni yoru shikin-chōtatsu 国債によ

る資金調達
deficit financing akaji-zai-sei 赤字財政
self-financing jiko-kin'yū 自己金融
fire *v.* kaiko-suru 解雇する
fire fighting toraburu o kai-ketsu-suru kinkyū-sochi トラブルを解決する緊急措置
firing kaiko 解雇
hiring and firing koyō oyobi kaiko 雇用および解雇
first-line manager dai-issen-kantoku 第一線監督
fiscal drag zaiseiteki-shōgai 財政的障害
fiscal policy zaisei-seisaku 財政政策
fiscal year kaikei-nendo 会計年度
fixed assets kotei-shisan 固定資産
fixed costs kotei-hiyō 固定費用
flexible budget danryokusei-yosan 弾力性予算
flexible firm tekiōsei no aru kigyō 適応性のある企業
flexible working hours dan-ryokuteki-kinmu-jikansei 弾力的勤務時間制
flexitime jikan-shinshuku-shukkinsei 時間伸縮出勤制
floppy furoppī フロッピー
floppy disk (floppy) furoppī-disuku フロッピーディスク
flotation shinhakkō-shōken no uri-dashi 新発行証券の売り出し
flow:
cash flow genkin-ryūdō 現金流動
discounted cash flow (DCF) genkin-shūshi-wari-biki(hō) 現金収支割引(法)
funds flow shikin-furō 資金フロー
incremental cash flow zōbun-genkin-furō 増分現金フロー
information flow jōhō no nagare 情報の流れ
flow chart sagyō-kōteizu 作業工程図
data flow chart dētā-keirozu データー経路図
flow diagram nagare-sagyōzu 流れ作業図
flow line kōtei-nagarezu 工程流れ図
flow process chart nagare-sagyō-kōteizu 流れ作業工程図
flow production nagare-sagyō-seisan 流れ作業生産
FMCG (fast-moving consumer goods) kōkaiten-shōhi-busshi 高回転消費物資
focus *v.* shōten o awaseru 焦点を合わせる
focus shōten 焦点
follower:
price follower kakaku-tsuizuisha 価格追随者
follow up *v.* tsuiseki-suru 追跡する
follow-up tsuiseki-chōsa 追跡調査
force:
sales force hanbairyoku 販売力
task force tasuku-fōsu タスクフォース
forces:
market forces shijō no chikara 市場の力

forecast yosoku 予測
budget forecast yosan-mitōshi 予算見通し
market forecast shijō-yosoku 市場予測
sales forecast hanbai-yosoku 販売予測
technological forecast gijutsu-yosoku 技術予測
forecasting yosoku 予測
budget forecasting yosan-yosoku 予算予測
business forecasting keiki-yosoku 景気予測
demand forecasting juyō-yosoku 需要予測
environmental forecasting kankyō-yosoku 環境予測
manpower forecasting dōin-kanō-jinteki-shigen-yosoku 動員可能人的資源予測
staff forecasting shokuin-mitōshi 職員見通し
foreman kantoku 監督
formation:
capital formation shihon-keisei 資本形成
strategy formation sen-ryaku-keisei 戦略形成
forward exchange rate sakimono-kawase-sōba 先物為替相場
forward market sakimono-shijō 先物市場
forward planning chōki-shi-harai-keikaku 長期支払計画
forward rate sakimono-sōba 先物相場
forward swap sakimono-suwappu 先物スワップ
fractionalize *v.* bunkatsu-suru 分割する
franchise *v.* eigyō-menkyo o ataeru 営業免許を与える
franchise eigyō-menkyo 営業免許
freelance (to go) jiyū-keiyaku (ni naru) 自由契約（になる）
freelance jiyūkeiyaku 自由契約
freeze *v.* tōketsu-suru 凍結する
freeze:
wage freeze chingin-tōketsu 賃金凍結
frequency distribution dosū-bunpu 度数分布
fringe benefits kōsei-kyūfu 厚生給付
fringe market shūhen-shijō 周辺市場
front-line employees dai-issen-jūgyōin 第一線従業員
full capacity zennōryoku 全能力
full-time employee jōkinsha 常勤者
full-time employment jōkinkoyō 常勤雇用
full-timer jōkinsha 常勤者
function kinō 機能
managerial function kanri-kinō 管理機能
function key kinō-kī 機能キー
functional kinōteki 機能的
functional analysis kinō-bunseki 機能分析
functional approach kinō-bunseki 機能分析
functional approval kinōteki-kakunin 機能的確認
functional costing kinō-kosuto (-keisan) 機能コスト（計算）
functional layout kinōteki-haichi 機能的配置

functional management shokumu-kanri 職務管理
functional organization shokunō-soshiki 職能組織
functional relations shokunō-kankei 職能関係
functional responsibility shokumu-sekinin 職務責任
fund:
sinking fund gensai-kikin 減債基金
slush fund fusei-shikin 不正資金
funding chōki-saika 長期債化
funds:
source and disposition of funds shikin-un'yōhyō 資金運用表
futures sakimono-torihiki 先物取引
financial futures kin'yū-saki-mono-torihiki 金融先物取引
futures market sakimono-shijō 先物市場

G

gain:
capital gain shihonteki-rijun 資本的利潤
game:
business game bijinesu-gēmu ビジネスゲーム
management game manējimento-gēmu マネージメントゲーム
game theory gēmu no riron ゲームの理論
gap study kakusa-kenkyū 格差研究
gateway gēto'uei ゲートウエイ
gathering:
data gathering shiryō-shūshū 資料収集
GDP (gross domestic product) kokunai-sōseisan 国内総生産
gearing dendō-sōchi 伝動装置
general glut zenmenteki-kajō-seisan 全面的過剰生産
generate ideas *v.* kikaku o umu 企画を生む
generic sōshō 総称
gentleman's agreement shinshi-kyōtei 紳士協定
gilt shichiya 質屋
gilt-edged security ichiryū-shōken 一流証券
gilt-edged stock yūryō-kabu 優良株
global image sekaiteki-imēji 世界的イメージ
global marketing sekai-shijō 世界市場
globalization sekaika 世界化
globalize *v.* sekaika-suru 世界化する
GNP (gross national product) kokumin-sōseisan 国民総生産
go public *v.* kabushiki o kōbo-suru 株式を公募する
go-getting sekkyokuteki na katsudō 積極的な活動
go-slow sabotāju サボタージュ
goal:
company goal kigyō-mokuteki 企業目的
profit goal rieki-mokuhyō 利益目標
sales goal hanbai-mokuhyō 販売目標
goals:
hierarchy of goals mokuhyō no yūsen-jun'i 目標の優先順位
goal-seeking mokuhyō-tassei 目標達成
goal-setting mokuhyō-settei 目標設定
going rate genkō-kinri 現行金利
golden handshake kanbu-shokuin no kaiko 幹部職員の解雇
golden hello saiyōji-tokubetsu-bōnasu 採用時特別ボーナス
golden parachute kanbu-shokuin no kaiko-teate 幹部職員の解雇手当
golden share sai-yūryō-kabu 最優良株
goods:
brown goods daidokoro-yō-igai no denki-seihin 台所用以外の電器製品

capital goods shihonzai 資本財
consumer goods shōhizai 消費財
convenience goods nichi-yōhin 日用品
durable goods taikyūzai 耐久財
fast-moving consumer goods (FMCG) kōkaiten-shōhi-busshi 高回転消費物資
impulse goods shōdōgai-shōhin 衝動買い商品
industrial goods seisanzai 生産財
investment goods tōshizai 投資財
non-durable goods hi-taikyūzai 非耐久財
white goods daidokoro-yō-denki-seihin 台所用電器製品
goodwill eigyō-ken 営業権
grade:
salary grade kyūyo-tōkyū 給与等級
grapevine gurēpu-bain グレープ・バイン
graphical user interface (GUI) zushiki-shiyōsha-intāfēsu 図式使用者インターフェース
graphics zukei 図形
green issues kankyō-mondai 環境問題
greenmail kabushiki o kai-atsume, kaisha ni kaitorasete rieki o eru 株式を買い集め、会社に買い取らせて利益を得る
grey market utagawashii tori-hiki 疑わしい取り引き
grid:
managerial grid manējaru-guriddo マネージャルグリッド
grid structure kōshi-kōzō 格子構造
grievance procedure kujō-shori (-tetsuzuki) 苦情処理（手続き）
gross domestic product (GDP) kokunai-sōseisan 国内総生産
gross margin (GM) sōrieki 総利益
gross national product (GNP) kokumin-sōseisan 国民総生産
gross profit sōrijun 総利潤
group accounts sōgō-zaimu-hyō 総合財務表
group bonus dantai-shōyo 団体賞与
group dynamics shūdan-rikigaku 集団力学
group incentive dantai-shōreikyū(-seido) 団体奨励給（制度）
group training dantai-kunren 団体訓練
T-group training tī-gurūpu-kunren ティーグループ訓練
growth:
corporate growth kigyō no seichō 企業の成長
organic growth yūkiteki-seichō 有機的成長
personal growth kojinteki-seichō 個人的成長
growth area seichō-chiiki 成長地域
growth index seichō-shisū 成長指数
growth industry seichō-sangyō 成長産業

growth potential senzai-seichōryoku 潜在成長力
growth strategy seichō-senryaku 成長戦略
guesstimate *v.* suisoku-suru 推測する
guesstimate suisokuteki-kettei 推測的決定
GUI (graphical user interface) zushiki-shiyōsha-intāfēsu 図式使用者インターフェース
guideline shidō-kijun 指導基準

H

hacker konpyūta-yaburi コンピュータ破り
hacking tsūjō-unten 通常運転
halo effect nanahikari-kōka 七光効果
handcuffs:
golden handcuffs kanbu-shokuin o tano soshiki no shikarubeki chiini oiyaru koto 幹部職員を他の組織のしかるべき地位に追いやること
handling:
information handling jōhō-shori 情報処理
materials handling unpan-kanri 運搬管理
handshake:
golden handshake kanbu-shokuin no kaiko 幹部職員の解雇
hands-on operation choku-setsu-kanshō-kanri 直接干渉管理
harassment:
sexual harassment seiteki-iyagarase 性的いやがらせ
hard copy hādo-kopī ハード・コピー
hard disk hādo-disuku ハード・ディスク
hard ecu kōkan-kanō no ōshū-tsūka 交換可能の欧州通貨
hard landing kō-chakuriku 硬着陸
hard sell gōin na urikata 強引な売り方
hard selling gōin na hanbai 強引な販売
hardware hādo'uea ハードウエア
harmonization chōwa-zukuri 調和作り
harmonize *v.* chōwa-saseru 調和させる
hazard:
occupational hazard shokugyōjō no kiken 職業上の危険
hazchem (hazardous chemicals) kiken na kagaku-kagō-butsu 危険な化学化合物
head office honsha 本社
head-hunt *v.* jinzai o atsumeru 人材を集める
head-hunter jinzai-boshū-gakari 人材募集係
head-hunting jinzai-chōtatsu 人材調達
hedge *v.* tsunagi-uri-suru つなぎ売りする
hedging tsunagi-baibai つなぎ売買
hedging operation kake-tsu-nagi-sōsa かけつなぎ操作
hello:
golden hello saiyōji-toku-betsu-bōnasu 採用時特別ボーナス
heuristics tansaku-hōhō 探索方法
hidden agenda himitsu-kyōgi-jikō 秘密協議事項
hidden assets bogai-shisan 簿外資産
hierarchy of goals mokuteki no jun'i 目的の順位
high-flier takanekabu 高値株
hire *v.* yatou 雇う
direct hire chokusetsu-koyō

直接雇用
plant hire kōjō-chintairyō 工場賃貸料
hiring and firing koyō oyobi kaiko 雇用および解雇
hold margins *v.* tesūryō o toru 手数料を取る
holding company mochikabu-gaisha 持ち株会社
holidays:
staggered holidays kōtai-kyūjitsu 交代休日
home country jikoku 自国
horizontal integration suihei-teki-gappei 水平的合併
host country aitekoku 相手国
hot money hotto-manē ホット・マネー
house style jisha no yarikata 自社のやり方
HRM (human resource management) jinteki-shigen-kanri 人的資源管理
human engineering ningen-kōgaku 人間工学
human relations ningen-kankei 人間関係
human resource development (HRD) jinteki-shigen-kaihatsu 人的資源開発
human resource management (HRM) jinteki-shigen-kanri 人的資源管理
human resource planning (HRP) jinteki-shigen-keikaku 人的資源計画
human resources jinteki-shigen 人的資源
hustle *v.* sekkyokuteki ni hataraku 積極的に働く
hygiene factors eisei-yōin 衛生要因
hype kodai-senden 誇大宣伝

I

idle capacity yūkyū-shisetsu 遊休施設
image:
brand image burando-imēji ブランドイメージ
corporate image kigyō-imēji 企業イメージ
global image zenchikyūteki-imēji 全地球的イメージ
product image seihin-imēji 製品イメージ
imaging ketsuzō 結像
imbalance:
trade imbalance bōeki-fukinkō 貿易不均衡
impact eikyō 影響
profit impact rieki-kōka 利益効果
implement *v.* jisshi-suru 実施する
implementation:
strategy implementation senryaku-jisshi 戦略実施
implication:
profit implication rieki-renrui 利益連類
import yu'nyū 輸入
parallel import heikō-yunyū 平行輸入
improvement:
job improvement shokumu no kaizen 職務の改善
product improvement seihin-kaizen 製品改善
profit improvement rieki-kaizen 利益改善
impulse shōdō 衝動
impulse buying shōdō-gai 衝動買い
impulse goods shōdō-gai-shōhin 衝動買い商品
impulse sale shōdō-uri 衝動売り
in-company shanai (teki) 社内（的）
in-depth interview shinsō-mensetsuhō 深層面接法
in-house shanai 社内
in-plant training kōjō-nai-kunren 工場内訓練
incentive shigeki 刺激
financial incentive kin'yūteki-shigeki 金融的刺激
group incentive dantai-shōrei kyū (-seido) 団体奨励給（制度）
tax incentive zeisei-jō no yūgū-sochi 税制上の優遇措置
incentive scheme shōrei-seido 奨励制度
income shotoku 所得
disposable income kashobun-shotoku 可処分所得
real income jisshitsu-shotoku 実質所得
income tax shotoku-zei 所得税
negative income tax mainasu-shotoku-zei マイナス所得税
incremental zōka-bun no 増加分の
incremental cash flow zōbun-genkin-furō 増分現金フロー
index:
consumer price index shōhisha-kakaku-shisū 消費者

価格指数
growth index seichō-shisū 成長指数
retail price index (RPI) kouri-kakaku-shisū 小売り価格指数
index number shihyō-sūji 指標数字
indicator:
performance indicator sagyō-shisū 作業指数
indirect costs kansetsu-hiyō 間接費用
indirect expenses kansetsuhi 間接費
indirect labour kansetsu-rōdō (-hi) 間接労働（費）
induction kinōhō 帰納法
industrial action sangyō-katsudō 産業活動
industrial democracy sangyō-minshushugi 産業民主主義
industrial dispute rōdō-sōgi 労働争議
industrial dynamics kigyō-dōtaigaku 企業動態学
industrial engineering sangyō-kōgaku 産業工学
industrial espionage sangyō-supai 産業スパイ
industrial goods kōgyō-seihin 工業製品
industrial injury rōdō-saigai 労働災害
industrial psychology sangyō-shinrigaku 産業心理学
industrial relations rōshi-kankei 労使関係
industrial relations department rōshi-kankeibu 労使関係部
industrial safety sangyō-anzen 産業安全
industrial security kōgyō-saiken 工業債券
industrial waste sangyō-haikibutsu 産業廃棄物
industry:
growth industry seichō-sangyō 成長産業
training within industry (TWI) kigyōnai-kunren 企業内訓練
inflation:
cost-push inflation hiyō-appaku-infure 費用圧迫インフレ
demand-pull inflation juyō-infure 需要インフレ
inflationary pressure infure-atsuryoku インフレ圧力
informal organization hi-kōshiki-soshiki 非公式組織
informatics jōhō-kagaku 情報科学
information:
computerized information system (COINS) konpyūta ni yoru jōhō shisutemu コンピュータによる情報システム
control information seigyo-jōhō 制御情報
management information keiei-jōhō 経営情報
management information system (MIS) keiei-jōhō-shisutemu 経営情報システム
price-sensitive information kakaku o sayū-suru jōhō 価格を左右する情報
information flow jōhō no nagare 情報の流れ
information handling jōhō-

shori 情報処理
information retrieval jōhō-kensaku 情報検索
information system jōhō-shisutemu 情報システム
information technology jōhō-gijutsu 情報技術
information theory jōhō-riron 情報理論
infrastructure shakai-shihon 社会資本
injury:
industrial injury sangyō-saigai 産業災害
innovate *v.* kaikaku-suru 改革する
innovative kaikakuteki 改革的
innovatory kaikaku 改革
input inputto インプット
computer input nyūryoku-sōchi 入力装置
insider dealing insaidā-torihiki インサイダー取引
insider trading insaidā-torihiki インサイダー取引
inspection:
staff inspection jūgyōin-satei 従業員査定
intangible assets mukei-shisan 無形資産
integrate *v.* tōgō-suru 統合する
integrated:
computer integrated manufacturing (CIM) konpyūta-tōgō-seisan コンピュータ統合生産
integrated management system tōgōteki-keiei-jōhō-kanri-seido 統合的経営情報管理制度
integrated package tōgō-pakkēji 統合パッケージ
integrated project management (IPM) tōgō-keikaku-kanri 統合計画管理
integration tōgōka 統合化
interactive taiwashiki, kuri-kaeshi 対話式, 繰り返し
interactive process kurikaeshi-sagyō 繰り返し作業
interest:
controlling interest shihai-teki-riken 支配的利権
job interest shigoto no rieki 仕事の利益
majority interest tasū (ha) no rieki 多数（派）の利益
minority interest shōsū (ha) no rieki 少数（派）の利益
vested interest kakutei-kenri 確定権利
interface intāfēsu インターフェース
graphical user interface (GUI) zushiki-shiyōsha-intāfēsu 図式使用者インターフェース
inter-firm comparison keiei-hikaku 経営比較
interlocking directorate kennin-jūyakukai 兼任重役会
internal audit naibu-kansa 内部監査
internal rate of return (IRR) naibu-shūekiritsu 内部収益率
internalize *v.* naibu-chōtatsu-suru 内部調達する
internationalize *v.* kokusaika-suru 国際化する
interview:
in-depth interview shinsō-mensetsuhō 深層面接法
intuitive management

chokkanteki-kanri 直感的管理
inventory:
perpetual inventory kei-zoku-kiroku-tanaoroshi(-seido) 継続記録棚卸し（制度）
inventory control zaiko (hin)-kanri 在庫（品）管理
inventory turnover zaiko-kaiten-ritsu 在庫回転率
investment tōshi 投資
return on investment (ROI) tōshi-kōritsu 投資効率
investment analysis tōshi-bunseki 投資分析
investment appraisal tōshi-satei 投資査定
investment bank tōshi-ginkō 投資銀行
investment budget tōshi-yosan 投資予算
investment criteria tōshi-kijun 投資基準
investment goods tōshizai 投資財
investment management tōshi-kanri 投資管理
investment mix kongō-tōshi 混合投資
investment policy tōshi-hōshin 投資方針
investment programme tōshi-puroguramu 投資プログラム
invisibles mukei-shisan 無形資産
IPM (integrated project management) sōgōkeikaku-kanri 総合計画管理
IRR (internal rate of return) naibu-shūekiritsu 内部収益率
irregular market henchō-shikyō 変調市況
issue mondaiten 問題点
rights issue kabunushi-wariate-hakkō 株主割当発行
issued capital hakkōzumi-kabushiki-shihonkin 発行済み株式資本金
IT (information technology) jōhō-gijutsu 情報技術

J

JIT (just in time) jasuto-in-taimu ジャスト・イン・タイム
job gyōmu 業務
job analysis shokumu-bunseki 職務分析
job assignment shokumu 職務
job challenge kadai 課題
job classification shokumu-bunrui 職務分類
job description shokumu-kijutsuhyō 職務記述表
job design shokumu-sekkei 職務設計
job enlargement shokumu-kakudai 職務拡大
job enrichment shokumu-kyōka 職務強化
job evaluation shokumu-satei 職務査定
job expectation shokumujō no kitai 職務上の期待
job improvement shokumu no kaizen 職務の改善
job interest shokumu-ken'eki 職務権益
job opening kyūjin 求人
job opportunity koyō-kikai 雇用機会
job performance shokumu-suikō 職務遂行
job profile gyōmu-shōkai 業務紹介
job rotation haichi-tenkan 配置転換
job satisfaction shokumu no manzokudo 職務の満足度
job security shokumu-hoshō 職務保証
job-sharing shokumu-buntan 職務分担
job simplification shokumu no tanjunka 職務の単純化
job specification shokumu-meisaisho 職務明細書
jobbing rinji no shigoto 臨時の仕事
joint consultation rōshi-kyōgi 労使協議
joint negotiation gōdō-rōshi-kōshō 合同労使交渉
joint representation gōdō-daihyō (sei) 合同代表（制）
joint venture gōben-kigyō 合弁企業
joint venture company gōben-gaisha 合弁会社
junk bond janku-bondo ジャンク・ボンド
jurisdiction kankatsuken 管轄権
just in time (JIT) jasuto-in-taimu ジャスト・イン・タイム

K

key buying factor shuyō-kai-yōin 主要買い要因
key success factor shuyō-seikō-yōin 主要成功要因
know-how nouhau ノウハウ

L

labour rōdō 労働
direct labour chokusetsu-rōdō (-hi) 直接労働（費）
indirect labour kansetsu-rōdō (-hi) 間接労働（費）
semi-skilled labour han-jukurenkō 半熟練工
skilled labour jukurenkō 熟練工
unskilled labour mi-jukurenkō 未熟練工
labour costs rōmuhi 労務費
labour dispute rōshi-funsō 労使紛争
labour-intensive rōdō-shū-yakuteki 労働集約的
labour mobility rōdō-ryūdōsei 労働流動性
labour relations rōshi-kankei 労使関係
labour turnover rōdō-kaiten-ritsu 労働回転率
labourers rōdōsha 労働者
lag chien 遅延
lag response chien-kaitō 遅延回答
LAN (local area network) kyokuchi-tsūshinmō 局地通信網
landing chakuriku 着陸
hard landing kō-chakuriku 硬着陸
soft landing nan-chakuriku 軟着陸
language:
common language kyōtsūgo 共通語
computer language konpyūta-gengo コンピュータ言語
machine language kikai-gengo 機械言語
laptop rappu-toppu-shiki ラップトップ式
laptop computer rappu-toppu-shiki-konpyūta ラップトップ式コンピュータ
laser printer rēzā-purintā レザープリンター
lateral thinking suihei-shikō 水平思考
latest date saishū-kijitsu 最終期日
launch uchiage 打ち上げ
product launch shinseihin no uridashi 新製品の売り出し
launching kaishi 開始
laundering rondaringu, sentaku (fusei-na shikin no) ロンダリング，洗濯（不正な資金の）
lay off *v.* ichiji-kaiko-suru 一時解雇する
lay-off ichiji-kaiko 一時解雇
layout:
functional layout kinōteki-haichi 機能的配置
plant layout study kōjō-shisetsu-haichi-kenkyū 工場施設配置研究
process equipment layout seisan-kōtei-shisetsu no haichi 生産工程施設の配置
LDC (less developed country) teikaihatsu-koku 低開発国
lead shiki 指揮
lead time junbi-kikan 準備期間
leader shidōsha 指導者

loss-leader medama-shōhin 目玉商品
market leader shudōkabu 主導株
price leader kakaku-sendōsha 価格先導者
team leader tīmu-rīdā チーム・リーダー

leader merchandising otori-shōhin おとり商品

leadership shidōryoku 指導力

leading edge tachiagari-kukan 立ち上がり区間

leak morekuchi 漏れ口
security leak kimitsu no rōei 機密の漏洩

leapfrogging kaeru-tobi-sōba 蛙飛び相場

learning:
distance learning gakugai de no gakushū 学外での学習
open learning tsūshin-kyōiku (ni yoru gakushū) 通信教育（による学習）
programmed learning puroguramudo-gakushū プログラムド学習

learning curve gakushū-kyokusen 学習曲線

lease *v.* chingashi-suru 賃貸しする

lease-lend chintai 賃貸

lease or buy *v.* chintai mata wa kaitori 賃貸又は買取

leasing chintaishaku 賃貸借
equipment leasing setsubi no chintai 設備の賃貸

least-cost saishō-hiyō 最小費用

less developed country (LDC) teikaihatsu-koku 低開発国

level:
wage level chingin-suijun 賃金水準

level playing-field suihei-undōjō 水平運動場

leverage teko no sayō テコの作用

leveraged bid rebarejjido-biddo レバレッジド・ビッド

leveraged buyout (LBO) rebarejjido-baiauto レバレッジド・バイアウト

liabilities saimu 債務
current liabilities ryūdō-fusai 流動負債

liability:
asset liability management shisan-fusai-kanri 資産負債管理

liberalization jiyūka 自由化

licence menkyo 免許
under licence kyoka o ete 許可を得て

licence production *v.* raisensu-seisan o okonau ライセンス生産を行う

licensing:
cross-licensing kōgo-tokkyo-shiyōken 交互特許使用権

life:
economic life kinōteki-taiyō-nensū 機能的耐用年数
product life seihin-jumyō 製品寿命
product life expectancy seihin-jumyō-yosoku 製品寿命予測
shelf-life chozō-jumyō 貯蔵寿命

life cycle (*of a product*) (shōhin no) jumyō（商品の）寿命

lifestyle seikatsu-yōshiki 生活

様式
lifestyle packaging tokutei no seikatsu-yōshiki o taishō to shita kōkoku 特定の生活様式を対象とした広告
limitation:
damage limitation songai-baishō-kigen 損害賠償期限
line:
assembly line kumitate-rain 組立ライン
down the line kanzen ni 完全に
flow line nagare-keiro 流れ経路
on line onrain オンライン
product line seisan-rain 生産ライン
line and staff rain to sutaffu ラインとスタッフ
line assistant rain-ashisutanto ラインアシスタント
line authority kanrisha no ken-gen 管理者の権限
line executive rain-bumon no sekininsha ライン部門の責任者
line management rain-bumon no kanri ライン部門の管理
line manager rain-kantokusha ライン監督者
line of command meirei-keitō 命令系統
line organization rain-soshiki ライン組織
line production rain-seisan ライン生産
linear programming senkei-keikakuhō 線型計画法
linear responsibility sekinin-keitō 責任系統
liquid assets ryūdō-shisan 流動資産
liquidate *v.* kankin-suru 換金する
liquidation kaisan 解散
liquidity ratio ryūdōsei-hiritsu 流動性比率
listed jōjō (-shita) 上場（した）
listing jōjō 上場
literate:
computer literate konpyūta-jōhōriron コンピュータ情報理論
load:
work load hyōjun-sagyōryō 標準作業量
load factor kajū-bairitsu, fuka-ritsu 荷重倍率，負荷率
loan:
back-to-back loan sōsai-rōn 相殺ローン
parallel loan heikō-shakkan 平行借款
loan capital kashitsuke-shihon 貸付資本
loan stock tenkan-shasai 転換社債
local area network (LAN) kyokuchi-tsūshinmō 局地通信網
local content rules genchi-buhin-shiyō-kisoku 現地部品使用規則
localization genchika 現地化
location:
plant location kōjō-shozai-chi 工場所在地
lock-out kōjō-heisa 工場閉鎖
logistic process kōhō-shien (-tetsuzuki) 後方支援（手続き）
logistical kōhō-gyōmu no

後方業務の
logistics kōhō-shiengaku 後方支援学
logo kigō 企業
company logo kaisha no shinboru-māku 会社のシンボル・マーク
lombard kanekashi 金貸し
long-term planning chōki-keikaku 長期計画
loop:
closed loop tojita-rūpu 閉じたループ
loss:
capital loss kotei-shisan-baikyaku-zon 固定資産売却損
loss-leader otori-shōhin おとり商品
loss-maker rosu-mēkā ロスメーカー
losses:
bad-debt losses kashi-daore-sonshitsu 貸倒れ損失
low-cost commodity tei-kakaku-shōhin 低価格商品
low-flier teikakaku-kabu 低価格株
low-tech teigijutsu 低技術
loyalty:
brand loyalty burando ni taisuru kodawari ブランドに対するこだわり
lump sum ichiji-kin 一時金

M

M&A (mergers and acquisitions) kigyō no kyūshū-gappei 企業の吸収合併
machine code kikai-kōdo 機械コード
machine language kikai-gengo 機械言語
macro makuro マクロ
mail:
direct mail dairekuto-mēru ダイレクトメール
electronic mail (e-mail) denshi-yūbin 電子郵便
mail merge yūbin no shurui-betsu kuwake 郵便の種類別区分け
mail order tsūshin-hanbai 通信販売
mailbox yūbin-posuto 郵便ポスト
mainframe hontai 本体
maintenance:
planned maintenance kei-kakuteki-hoshu 計画的保守
preventive maintenance teikiteki-hoshu 定期的保守
productive maintenance seisanteki-setsubi-hozen 生産的設備保全
resale price maintenance (RPM) saihan-kakaku-iji (-sei-do) 再販価格維持（制度）
total plant maintenance sōgōteki-kōjō-hozen 総合的工場保全
majority interest tasū (ha) no rieki 多数（派）の利益
make-or-buy decision jisei ka kōnyū ka no kettei 自製か購入かの決定
maker:
market maker shijō-kai-hatsusha 市場開発者
malfunction kinō-furyō 機能不良
manage *v.* kanri-suru 管理する
managed:
system-managed company shisutemu-kanri-kigyō システム管理企業
managed costs kanri-kanō-hiyō 管理可能費用
management keiei (jin) 経営(陣)
asset liability management shisan-fusai-kanri 資産負債管理
asset management shisan-kanri 資産管理
business management kigyō-keiei 企業経営
cash management genkin-kanri 現金管理
change management henkō-kanri 変更管理
credit management shinyō-kanri 信用管理
crisis management kiki-kanri 危機管理
decentralized management bunkenteki-keiei 分権的経営
distribution management ryūtsū-kanri 流通管理
divisional management bumon-kanri 部門管理
dynamic management model dōtai-keiei-moderu 動態経営モデル
effective management kō-kateki-na kanri 効果的な管理

financial management zaimu-kanri 財務管理
functional management shokumu-kanri 職務管理
general management sōkatsu-kanri 総括管理
human resource management (HRM) jinteki-shigen-kanri 人的資源管理
integrated management system tōgōteki-keiei-jōhō-kanri-seido 統合的経営情報管理制度
integrated project management (IPM) tōgō-keikaku-kanri 統合計画管理
intuitive management chokkanteki-kanri 直感的管理
investment management tōshi-kanri 投資管理
line management rain-bumon no kanri ライン部門の管理
manpower management rōdōryoku-kanri 労働力管理
market management shijō-kanri 市場管理
matrix management matorikkusu-kanri マトリックス管理
middle management chū-kan-kanrishoku 中間管理職
multiple management takaku-keiei 多角経営
office management jimu-kanri 事務管理
operating management sagyō-kanri 作業管理
operations management jigyō-bumon-kanri 事業部門管理
participative management jūgyōin-sanka-keiei 従業員参加経営
personnel management jinji-kanri 人事管理
physical distribution management butteki-ryūtsū-kanri 流通管理
portfolio management shisan-kanri 資産管理
product management seisanbutsu-kanri 生産物管理
production management seisan-kanri 生産管理
programmed management proguramu-kanri プログラム管理
project management keikaku-kanri 計画管理
quality management hinshitsu-kanri 品質管理
resource management shigen-kanri 資源管理
risk management kiken-kanri 危険管理
safety management anzen-kanri 安全管理
sales management hanbai-kanri 販売管理
scientific management kagakuteki-kanri 科学的管理
staff management shokuin-kanri 職員管理
supervisory management kanshi-kanri 監視管理
systems management shi-sutemu-kanri システム管理
time management jikan-kanri 時間管理
top management saikō-keiei-sha 最高経営者
top management approach

saikō-keieisha-hōshiki 最高経営者方式
total quality management (TQM) tōgōteki-hinshitsu-kanri 統合的品質管理
venture management kiki-kanri 危機管理

management accounting kanri-kaikei 管理会計

management audit keiei-kansa 経営監査

management buyout (MBO) manējimento-baiauto マネージメント・バイアウト

management by exception reigai-kanri 例外管理

management by objectives (MBO) mokuhyō-kanri 目標管理

management chart kanri-zuhyō 管理図表

management consultancy keiei-konsarutanto-gyō 経営コンサルタント業

management consultant keiei-konsarutanto 経営コンサルタント

management contract keiei-keiyaku 経営契約

management development keieisha-keihatsu 経営者啓発

management efficiency keiei-kōritsu 経営効率

management game bijinesu-gēmu ビジネスゲーム

management information keiei-jōhō 経営情報

management information system (MIS) keiei-jōhō-shisutemu 経営情報システム

management potential keieisha no senzai-nōryoku 経営者の潜在能力

management practices keiei-kankō 経営慣行

management ratio keiei-hiritsu 経営比率

management science keiei-kagaku 経営科学

management services kanri-gyōmu 管理業務

management succession planning keiei-keishō-keikaku 経営継承計画

management system keiei-soshiki 経営組織

management team keiei-chīmu 経営チーム

management technique keiei-gijutsu 経営技術

management theory keiei-riron 経営理論

manager keieisha 経営者
advertising manager kōkoku-sekininsha 広告責任者
area manager chiiki-sekininsha 地域責任者
assistant manager fuku-shihainin 副支配人
assistant to manager shihainin no joshu 支配人の助手
brand manager burando-manējā ブランドマネージャー
departmental manager bumon-kanrisha 部門管理者
deputy manager shihainin-dairi 支配人代理
distribution manager hanbai-kanrisha 販売管理者
first-line manager daiissen-kantoku 第一線監督

general manager buchō 部長
line manager rain-kantoku-sha ライン監督者
marketing manager hanbai-sekininsha 販売責任者
operations manager sagyō-kanrisha 作業管理者
owner-manager ōnā-keiei-sha オーナー経営者
personnel manager jinji-tantōsha 人事担当者
plant manager kōjōchō 工場長
product manager seihin-kanrisha 製品管理者
production manager seisan-kanrisha 生産管理者
project manager purojekuto-manējā プロジェクト・マネージャー
purchasing manager kōnyū-kanrisha 購入管理者
sales manager hanbai-sekininsha 販売責任者
works manager sagyō-kanrisha 作業管理者

managerial kanri-sareta 管理された

managerial control kanriteki-tōsei 管理的統制

managerial effectiveness kanri-kōka 管理効果

managerial function kanri-kinō 管理機能

managerial grid manējaru-guriddo マネージャルグリッド

managerial structure kanri-kikō 管理機構

managerial style kanri-hōshiki 管理方式

managing director (MD) jōmu-torishimariyaku 常務取締役
deputy managing director jōmu-torishimariyaku-ho 常務取締役補

manned yūjin no 有人の

manning jin'in-haichi 人員配置

manpower jinzai 人材
executive manpower strategy kanrishoku (-kakutoku) -senryaku 管理職（獲得）戦略

manpower audit jin'inhyō 人員表

manpower forecasting rōdōryoku-yosō 労働力予想

manpower management rōdōryoku-kanri 労働力管理

manpower planning jin'in-keikaku 人員計画

manpower resourcing rōdōryoku-chōtatsu (gen) 労働力調達（源）

manufacture *v.* seizō-suru 製造する

manufacturing:
computer-integrated manufacturing (CIM) konpyūta-tōgō-seisan コンピュータ統合生産
economic manufacturing quantity saiteki-seisanryō 最適生産量

manufacturing capacity seisan-nōryoku 生産能力

manufacturing control seisan-kanri 生産管理

manufacturing cost seizōhi 製造費

margin:

gross margin (GM) ara-rieki 粗利益
net margin jun-rieki 純利益
profit margin shōkokin 証拠金
margin of safety anzen-yoyū-ritsu 安全余裕率
marginal analysis genkai-bunseki 限界分析
marginal costs genkai-hiyō 限界費用
marginal costing genkai-genka-keisan 限界原価計算
marginal efficiency genkai-kōritsu 限界効率
marginal pricing genkai-kakaku-kettei 限界価格決定
marginalize *v.* mushi-suru 無視する
margins:
hold margins *v.* rieki o iji-suru 利益を維持する
market *v.* shijō de baibai-suru 市場で売買する
market:
bear market yowaki-sōba 弱気相場
bull market kaite-sōba 買い手相場
buyers' market kaite-shijō 買い手市場
commodity market shōhin-shijō 商品市場
down-market sage-sōba 下げ相場
equity market kabushiki-shijō 株式市場
financial market kin'yū-shijō 金融市場
forward market sakimono-shijō 先物市場
fringe market shūhen-shijō 周辺市場
grey market utagawashii-torihiki 疑わしい取り引き
mature market seijuku-shijō 成熟市場
sellers' market urite-shijō 売り手市場
stock market shōken-shijō 証券市場
up-market jōshō-sōba 上昇相場
market appraisal shijō-hyōka 市場評価
market awareness shijō-ishiki 市場意識
market driven shijō-jōhō-ison 市場情報依存
market dynamics shijō-rikigaku 市場力学
market exploration shijō-chōsa 市場調査
market forces shijō no chikara 市場の力
market forecast shijō no yo-soku 市場の予測
market intelligence shijō (himitsu) -jōhō 市場(秘密)情報
market leader shudō-kabu 主導株
market maker shijō-kaihatsu-sha 市場開発者
market management shijō-kanri 市場管理
market opportunity torihiki-kikai 取引機会
market penetration shijō-sannyū 市場参入
market plan shijō-keikaku 市場計画
market potential shijō-senzai-ryoku 市場潜在力
market price shijō-kakaku 市

場価格
market profile shijō-purofīru 市場プロフィール
market prospects torihiki-yosoku 取引予測
market rating shijō-kinri 市場金利
market research shijō-chōsa 市場調査
market saturation shijō-shintō 市場浸透
market segment shijō-kubun 市場区分
market segmentation shijō-saibunka 市場細分化
market-sensitive shijō-fuan 市場不安
market share shijō-sen'yūritsu 市場占有率
market structure shijō-kōzō 市場構造
market study shijō-kenkyū 市場研究
market survey shijō-chōsa 市場調査
market test shijō-kensa 市場検査
market trend shijō-dōkō 市場動向
market value shijō-kachi 市場価値
marketable shijōsei no aru 市場性のある
marketing shijō-torihiki 市場取引
creative marketing sōzōteki-shijō 創造的市場
direct marketing choku-setsu-torihiki 直接取り引き
global marketing kokusai-torihiki 国際取り引き
niche marketing taishō o shibotta eigyō 対象をしぼった営業
test marketing jikken-shijō 実験市場
marketing appropriation shijō-un'yō 市場運用
marketing budget mākettingu-yosan マーケッティング予算
marketing manager hanbai-sekininsha 販売責任者
marketing mix mākettingu-mikkusu マーケッティングミックス
marketing research shijō-chōsa 市場調査
marketing strategy shijō-senryaku 市場戦略
mark-up niage 荷揚げ
mass:
critical mass genkairyō 限界量
mass production tairyō-seisan 大量生産
massage the figures *v.* sūji o sōsa-suru 数字を操作する
material:
point-of-sale material bup-pin-hanbai-jiten 物品販売時点
materials handling unpan-kanri 運搬管理
materials shiryō 資料
mathematical programming sūri-keikakuhō 数理計画法
matrix management mato-rikkusu-kanri マトリックス管理
matrix organization matori-kkusu-soshiki マトリックス組織
mature economy seijuku-kei-zai 成熟経済

mature market seijuku-shijō 成熟市場
maximization:
profit maximization rieki-kyokudaika 利益極大化
maximize *v.* saidaika-suru 最大化する
maximum product value seihin no saidai-kachi 製品の最大価値
MBO (management by objectives) mokuhyō-kanri 目標管理
mean shudan 手段
meaningful imi no aru 意味のある
measurement:
clerical work measurement jimu-jikan-sokutei 事務時間測定
performance measurement seinō-sokutei 性能測定
productivity measurement seisansei-sokutei 生産性測定
work measurement sagyō-sokutei 作業測定
media baitai 媒体
advertising media kōkoku-baitai 広告媒体
media analysis media-bunseki メディア分析
media selection baitai-sentaku 媒体選択
median chūōchi 中央値
mediate *v.* chūsai-suru 仲裁する
mediation chūsai 仲裁
meeting:
board meeting torishimari-yaku-kai 取締役会
memory kioku-sōchi 記憶装置
computer memory konpyūta-memorī コンピュータ・メモリー
computer memory chip konpyūta-memorī chippu コンピュータ・メモリー・チップ
random-access memory (RAM) tōsoku-yobidashi-kioku-sōchi 等速呼び出し記憶装置
read-only memory (ROM) kotei-kioku-sōchi 固定記憶装置
merchandising hanbai-sokushin-katsudō 販売促進活動
leader merchandising otori-shōryaku おとり商略
merchant bank shōgyō-ginkō 商業銀行
merge *v.* heigō-suru 併合する
merger gappei 合併
merit rating seiseki-hyōka 成績評価
message:
advertising message kōkoku-messēji 広告メッセージ
methectics shūdan-rikigaku 集団力学
method:
points-rating method tensū-hyōkahō 点数評価法
present value method genkahō 現価法
random observation method musakui-kansatsuhō 無作為観察法
simplex method tantaihō 単体法
method of simulation shimyurēshon-hō シミュレーション法
methods:

organization and methods (O & M) gyōmu-kaizen-katsu-dō 業務改善活動
time and methods study jikan oyobi hōhō-kenkyū 時間および方法研究
methods engineering hōhō-kōgaku 方法工学
methods study hōhō-kenkyū 方法研究
micro bishiteki 微視的
microchip maikuro-chippu マイクロ・チップ
middle management chūkan-kanrishoku 中間管理職
minimize risks *v.* kiken o kyokushōka-suru 危険を極小化する
minimum wage saitei-chingin 最低賃金
minority interest shōsū (ha) no rieki 少数（派）の利益
MIS (management information system) keiei-jōhō-chōsa-seido 経営情報調査制度
mission:
economic mission keizai-shisetsudan 経済使節団
mission statement gyōmu-sashizusho 業務指図書
mix:
investment mix tōshi-mikkusu 投資ミックス
marketing mix hanbai-yosō no ketsugō 販売予想の結合
product mix fukugō-seisan-butsu 複合生産物
promotional mix kaihatsu-yosō no ketsugō 開発予想の結合
sales mix hanbai-sokushin-yosō no ketsugō 販売促進予想の結合
mobile:
upwardly mobile jōhō e no idō 上方への移動
mobile phone idōshiki-denwa 移動式電話
mobility:
labour mobility rōdō-ryūdō-sei 労働流動性
staff mobility jūgyōin no ryūdōsei 従業員の流動性
mode yōshiki 様式
model moderu モデル
accounting model kaikei-moderu 会計モデル
corporate model kigyō-moderu 企業モデル
decision model ishikettei-moderu 意志決定モデル
dynamic management model dōtai-keiei-moderu 動態経営モデル
model analysis moderu-bunseki モデル分析
modem dētā-dentatsu-sōchi データー伝達装置
modular production mojurā-seisan モジュラー生産
modularity mojūru-sei モジュール性
monetarism manetarizumu マネタリズム
money supply tsūka-kyōkyū (ryō) 通貨供給（量）
monitor *v.* kanshi-suru 監視する
monitor performance *v.* sagyō o kanshi-suru 作業を監視する
monitoring:
performance monitoring sagyō-kanshi 作業監視

moonlighting fukugyō 副業
morphological analysis keitai-bunseki 形態分析
motion:
predetermined motion time system (PMTS) yotei-dōsa-jikan-hōshiki 予定動作時間方式
time and motion study jikan oyobi dōsa no kenkyū 時間および動作の研究
motion economy dōsa-keizai 動作経済
motion study dōsa-kenkyū 動作研究
motivate *v.* dōki o ataeru 動機を与える
motivation dōki 動機
motivational research dōki-chōsa 動機調査
motivator dōki-zuke-suru mono 動機づけするもの
motive:
profit motive rijun-dōki 利潤動機
mouse mausu (konpyūta no shiji-kiki) マウス（コンピュータの指示機器）
MRA (multiple regression analysis) tajū-kaiki-bunseki 多重回帰分析
multi-access tajū-shori 多重処理
multimedia training maruchi-media-kunren マルチメディア訓練
multiple management taka-ku-keiei 多角経営
multiple regression analysis (MRA) tajū-kaiki-bunseki 多重回帰分析
mutual recognition sōgo-hyōka 相互評価

N

name of the game gēmu no namae ゲームの名前
natural wastage shizen-sonmō 自然損耗
need-to-know basis kijun-rikai no gimu 基準理解の義務
needs analysis nīzu-bunseki ニーズ分析
training needs analysis kunren-nīzu-bunseki 訓練ニーズ分析
negative cash flow fusai no ryūdō 負債の流動
negative debt shihon 資本
negative income tax gyaku-shotoku-zei 逆所得税
negotiate *v.* kōshō-suru 交渉する
negotiation:
joint negotiation gōdō-rōshi-kōshō 合同労使交渉
negotiation strategy kōshō-senryaku 交渉戦略
net assets junshisan 純資産
net capital junshihon 純資本
net current assets shōmi-ryūdō-shisan 正味流動資産
net margin junrieki 純利益
net present value (NPV) shōmi-genka 正味現価
net profit jun'eki 純益
net worth jiko-shihon 自己資本
network *v.* nettowāku o tsukuru ネットワークを作る
network:
communications network tsūshinmō 通信網
distribution network ryū-tsū-kikō 流通機構
information network jōhō-mō 情報網
open network provision kaihōshiki-tsūshinmō setsubi 開放式通信網設備
wide area network (WAN) kōiki-nettowāku 広域ネットワーク
network analysis nettowāku-bunseki ネットワーク分析
networking nettowāku-zukuri ネットワーク作り
new-product development shinseihin-kaihatsu 新製品開発
newly industrialized country (NIC) shinkō-sangyō-koku 新興産業国
NIC (newly industrialized country) shinkō-sangyō-koku 新興産業国
niche katsudō-han'i 活動範囲
niche marketing taishō o shi-botta eigyō 対象をしぼった営業
night shift yakin 夜勤
no-strike clause sutoraiki-kin-shi-jōkō ストライキ禁止条項
nominal wages meimoku-chingin 名目賃金
non-durable goods hi-tai-kyūzai 非耐久財
non-executive director hijōkin-torishimariyaku 非常勤取締役
non-linear programming hi-senkei-keikakuhō 非線形計画法
non-price factors hi-kakaku-

teki-yōin 非価格的要因
non-profit-making hi-eiri 非営利
non-verbal communication hi-gengo-komyunikēshon 非言語コミュニケーション
NPV (net present value) shōmi-genka 正味現価
NTB (non-tariff barrier) hikanzei-shōheki 非関税障壁
number-crunching jūgyōin-sakugen 従業員削減
numbers game nanbāsu-gēmu ナンバース・ゲーム
numerical control sūchi-sei-gyo 数値制御

O

O & M (organization and methods) gyōmu-kaizen-katsudō 業務改善活動
objective mokuteki 目的
company objective kigyō-mokuteki 企業目的
objectives:
management by objectives (MBO) mokuhyō-kanri 目標管理
overall company objectives kigyō no sōgōteki na mokuteki 企業の総合的な目的
performance against objectives mokuteki ni hansuru tasseido 目的に反する達成度
objective-setting mokuhyō-settei 目標設定
observation:
random observation method musakui-kansatsuhō 無作為観察法
obsolescence chinpuka 陳腐化
built-in obsolescence kōzō-teki-chinpuka 構造的陳腐化
planned obsolescence keikakuteki-chinpuka 計画的陳腐化
occupational hazard shokugyōteki na kiken 職業的な危険
off line hi-chokketsu 非直結
off stream hi-renzoku 非連続
off-the-job training shokuba-gai-kunren 職場外訓練
office:
branch office shisha 支社
design office sekkei-jimusho 設計事務所
electronic office denshika-sareta-jimusho 電子化された事務所
head office honsha 本社
office automation jimu-jidōka 事務自動化
office automation design jimusho no sekkei 事務所の設計
office management jimu-kanri 事務管理
office planning jimu-kaizen-keikaku 事務改善計画
officer:
training officer kunren-tantōsha 訓練担当者
offshore okiai 沖合
offshore investment kaigai-tōshi 海外投資
on line chokketsu 直結
on stream renzoku 連続
one-off kobetsu-seisan 個別生産
ongoing shinkō-chū no 進行中の
open-ended kaihōshiki no 開放式の
open learning tsūshin-kyōiku (ni yoru gakushū) 通信教育（による学習）
open network provision kaihōshiki-tsūshinmō-setsubi 開放式通信網設備
open plan kaihō-keikaku 開放計画
open shop ōpun-shoppu オープンショップ
operating division jigyō-bumon 事業部門

operating management gyōmu-kanri 業務管理
operational sōsa-kanō na 操作可能な
operational planning gyōmu-keikaku 業務計画
operational research (OR) gyōmu-chōsa 業務調査
operations jigyō-bumon 事業部門
ancillary operations hojoteki-sagyō 補助的作業
hedging operations tsunagi-sōsa つなぎ操作
operations audit gyōmu-kansa 業務監査
operations breakdown gyōmu-bunseki 業務分析
operations management jigyō-bumon-kanri 事業部門管理
operations manager sagyō-kanri (sha) 作業管理（者）
operations manpower dōin-kanō-jin'in 動員可能人員
operations research (OR) gyōmu-chōsa 業務調査
opportunity:
equal employment opportunity byōdō-koyō-kikai 平等雇用機会
market opportunity torihiki-kikai 取引機会
window of opportunity kansatsu no kikai 観察の機会
opportunity costs kikai-hiyō 機会費用
optimal condition saiteki-jōken 最適条件
optimal output saiteki-seisanryō 最適生産量
optimal price saiteki-kakaku 最適価格
optimization:
profit optimization rijun-saitekika 利潤最適化
option:
stock option kabushiki-kaiire-sentakuken 株式買い入れ選択権
stock option plan kabushiki-yūsen-kaitori-sentakuken (-seido) 株式優先買取選択権(制度)
traded option baikyaku-zumi no sentakuken 売却済の選択権
OR (operational research) gyōmu-chōsa 業務調査
order:
economic order quantity saiteki-hatchūryō 最適発注量
organic growth kigyō-zentai no seichō 企業全体の成長
organigram soshiki-kiroku 組織記録
organization soshiki 組織
functional organization shokunō-soshiki 職能組織
informal organization hi-kōshiki-soshiki 非公式組織
line organization rain-soshiki ライン組織
matrix organization mato-rikkusu-soshiki マトリックス組織
staff organization sutaffu-soshiki スタッフ組織
organization and methods (O & M) gyōmu-kaizen-katsudō 業務改善活動
organization chart soshikizu 組織図
organization culture soshiki-

bunka 組織文化
organization planning setsuritsu-keikaku (-ritsuan) 設立計画（立案）
organization structure soshiki-kōsei 組織構成
organization theory soshikiron 組織論
organizational behaviour soshikiteki-kōdō 組織的行動
organizational change soshikiteki na henkō 組織的な変更
organizational development soshikiteki na hatten 組織的な発展
organizational effectiveness soshikiteki-kōka 組織的効果
organizational slack soshiki-yoyū 組織余裕
organogram hōhōronteki-gensoku-shugi 方法論的原則主義
orientation:
consumer orientation kokyaku-shikō 顧客志向
customer orientation kokyaku-jōhō-teikyō 顧客情報提供
out-house shagai 社外
outlook:
business outlook bijinesu-mitōshi ビジネス見通し
profit outlook rieki-mitōshi 利益見通し
outplacement gaibu-haichi 外部配置
output shutsuryoku 出力
capital-output ratio shihon-keisū 資本係数
input-output analysis tōnyū-sanshutsu-bunseki 投入産出分析
input-output table tōnyū-sanshutsuhyō 投入産出表
output budgeting sanshutsu-yosan 産出予算
output effect sanshutsuryō-kōka 産出量効果
outside director shagai-jūyaku 社外重役
outsourcing shagai-chōtatsu 社外調達
OVA (overhead value analysis) kansetsuhi-kachi-bunseki 間接費価値分析
overall company objectives kigyō no tōgōteki na mokuteki 企業の統合的な目的
overcapacity kajō-seisan-nōryoku 過剰生産能力
overcapitalized kadai-shihon-ka (sareta) 過大資本化（された）
overextended kajō-kakudai 過剰拡大
overhead value analysis (OVA) sōkeihi-kachi-bunseki 総経費価値分析
overheads keihi 経費
administrative overheads kanri-sho-keihi 管理諸経費
factory overheads kōjō-keihi 工場経費
overheads recovery keihi-kaishū 経費回収
overmanned kajō-jin'in-haichi 過剰人員配置
overmanning jin'in-kajō 人員過剰
overprice *v.* takane o tsukeru 高値をつける
overstaffing kajō-shokuin-koyō 過剰職員雇用
overtime zangyō 残業
owner-manager shashu-keiei-sha 社主経営者

P

package (a policy) *v.* ikkatsu-suru 一括する

package:

integrated package tōgō-pakkēji 統合パッケージ

software package sofutouea-pakkēji ソフトウェア・パッケージ

package deal hōkatsu-kōshō 包括交渉

packaging hōsō 包装

palletization paretto-yusō パレット輸送

panel:

consumers' panel shōhi-sha-meibo 消費者名簿

par gakumen 額面

above par gakumen-ijō 額面以上

at par gakumen de 額面で

parachute:

golden parachute kanbu-shokuin no kaiko-teate 幹部職員の解雇手当

parallel currency heikō-tsūka 平行通貨

parallel import heikō-yunyū 平行輸入

parallel loan heikō-shakkan 平行借款

parameter paramētā パラメーター

parametric programming parametarikku-keisan パラメタリック計算

parent company oya-gaisha 親会社

part-analysis training bunsan-kunren 分散訓練

part-time employment hi-jōkin-jūgyōin no koyō 非常勤従業員の雇用

part-timer hi-jōkin-jūgyōin 非常勤従業員

participation sanka 参加

worker participation jūgyōin no keiei-sanka 従業員の経営参加

participative management jūgyōin-sanka-keiei 従業員参加経営

partner kyōdō-keieisha 共同経営者

partnership kyōdō-keiei 共同経営

party:

working party shigoto-naka-ma 仕事仲間

patent tokkyo (-ken) 特許(権)

patent trading tokkyo-baibai 特許売買

pay:

equal pay dōitsu-chingin 同一賃金

profit-related pay rijun-bunpai-kyūyo 利潤分配給与

severance pay taishokukin 退職金

take-home pay tedori-kyūryō 手取り給料

pay-as-you-earn (PAYE) dekidaka-barai 出来高払い

pay-as-you-go genkin-barai (-shugi) 現金払い（主義）

pay-off kaiko 解雇

pay pause chingin-tōketsu 賃金凍結

pay round kyūyo-kikan 給与期間

pay talks chingin-kōshō 賃金交渉
payback gankin-kaishū 元金回収
payback period kaishū-kikan 回収期間
payment:
ex gratia **payment** mimaikin 見舞金
payment by results nōritsu-kyū 能率給
payroll chingin-meisaihyō 賃金明細表
payroll deduction kyūyo-kōjo 給与控除
PC (personal computer) pasokon パソコン
P/E (price-earnings ratio) kabuka-shūekiritsu 株価収益率
penetration:
market penetration shijō-sannyū 市場参入
penetration pricing shijō-shintō-kakaku(-seisaku) 市場浸透価格（政策）
per-share earnings hitokabu atari no shūeki 一株当たりの収益
performance:
earnings performance shūeki-gyōseki 収益業績
job performance shigoto no jikkō 仕事の実行
monitor performance *v.* sagyō o kanshi-suru 作業を監視する
product performance seihin-seinō 製品性能
profit performance shūeki-gyōseki 収益業績
share price performance hito-kabu-atari no kakaku to seinō no taihi 一株当たりの価格と性能の対比
standard performance hyōjun-sagyō 標準作業
performance against objectives mokuhyō ni hansuru tasseido 目標に反する達成度
performance appraisal gyōseki-hyōka 業績評価
performance budgeting gyōmu-yosan (-sakusei) 業務予算（作成）
performance evaluation gyōmu-hyōka 業務評価
performance indicator sagyō-shisū 作業指数
performance measurement gyōseki-sokutei 業績測定
performance monitoring sagyō-kanshi 作業監視
performance rating tasseido-satei 達成度査定
performance review nōritsu-kensa 能率検査
performance standard gyōseki-kijun 業績基準
peripheral equipment shūhen-sōchi 周辺装置
peripherals shūhen-sōchi 周辺装置
perpetual inventory keizoku-kiroku-tanaoroshi (-seido) 継続記録棚卸し（制度）
personal computer (PC) pasokon パソコン
personal growth jinteki-seichō 人的成長
personalize *v.* kojin-senyō ni suru 個人専用にする
personnel department jinjibu 人事部

personnel management jinji-kanri 人事管理
personnel manager jinji-tantōsha 人事担当者
personnel policy jinji-hōshin 人事方針
personnel rating jinji-kōsa 人事考査
personnel specification jūgyōin-shikakusho 従業員資格書
PERT (programme evaluation and review technique) pātohō パート法
pertinence tree naiyō-kanrenzu 内容関連図
petty cash koguchi-genkin 小口現金
petty expenses zappi 雑費
phase:
time phase jikan no jōkyō 時間の状況
phase in *v.* dankaiteki ni dō-nyū-suru 段階的に導入する
phase out *v.* dankaiteki ni hai-shi-suru 段階的に廃止する
philosophy:
company philosophy kigyō-tetsugaku 企業哲学
physical distribution management butteki-ryūtsū-kanri 物的流通管理
picket miharinin 見張り人
pie chart bun'enzu 分円図
piecework ukeoi-shigoto 請負仕事
pilot production shikenteki-seisan 試験的生産
pioneer *v.* kaitaku-suru 開拓する
pioneer product shisakuhin 試作品
piracy tokkyoken-shingai 特許権侵害
plan:
action plan kōdō-hōshin 行動方針
market plan shijō-keikaku 市場計画
open plan kōkai-keikaku 公開計画
share of production plan seisan-buntan-keikaku 生産分担計画
stock option plan kabushiki-yūsen-kaitori-sentakuken (-seido) 株式優先買取選択権（制度）
tactical plan senjutsuteki-kunren (-keikaku) 戦術的訓練（計画）
planned maintenance keikakuteki-hoshu 計画的保守
planned obsolescence keikakuteki-chinpuka 計画的陳腐化
planning keikaku (-sakutei) 計画（策定）
career planning keireki-keikaku 経歴計画
company planning kigyō-keikaku (-ritsuan) 企業計画（立案）
contingency planning saigai-taisaku 災害対策
departmental planning bumonbetsu-keikaku 部門別計画
distribution planning hanbai-keikaku 販売計画
financial planning zaimu-keikaku 財務計画
human resource planning

(HRP) jinteki-shigen-keikaku 人的資源計画
long-range planning chōki-keizai-keikaku 長期経済計画
long-term planning chōki-keikaku 長期計画
manpower planning jin'in-keikaku 人員計画
office planning jimu-kaizen-keikaku 事務改善計画
operational planning jigyō-keikaku 事業計画
organization planning soshiki-keikaku (-sakutei) 組織計画（策定）
product planning seihin-keikaku 製品計画
production planning seisan-keikaku 生産計画
production planning and control seisan-keikaku-kanri 生産計画管理
profit planning rijun-keikaku 利潤計画
project planning kikaku-sakutei 企画策定
sales planning hanbai-keikaku 販売計画
short-term planning tanki-keikaku 短期計画
staff planning shokuin (saiyō)-keikaku 職員（採用）計画
strategic planning senryakuteki-keikaku 戦略的計画
succession planning kōkeisha-keikaku 後継者計画
systems planning shisutemu-keikaku システム計画

planning department kikakubu 企画部
planning, programming, budgeting system (PPBS) kikaku-keikaku-yosan-settei 企画計画予算設定
plant bargaining kōjō-betsu-kōshō 工場別交渉
plant capacity seizō-nōryoku 製造能力
plant hire seisan-shisetsu no chingashi 生産施設の賃貸し
plant layout study kōjō-haichi-kenkyū 工場配置研究
plant location kōjō-shozaichi 工場所在地
plant maintenance kōjō-hoshu 工場保守
total plant maintenance tōgōteki-kōjō-hoshu 統合的工場保守
plant manager kōjōchō 工場長
player:
team player soshiki no ichi-in 組織の一員
ploughback rieki no saitōshi 利益の再投資
PMTS (predetermined motion time system) yotei-dōsa-jikan-hōshiki 予定動作時間方式
point:
breakdown point son'eki-bunkiten 損益分岐点
point-of-sale (POS) hanbai-jiten 販売時点
point-of-sale advertising hanbai-kasho-senden 販売箇所宣伝
point-of-sale material buppin-hanbai-kasho 物品販売箇所

points-rating method tensū-hyōkahō 点数評価法
poison pill dokuyaku 毒薬
policy:
business policy eigyō-seisaku 営業政策
company policy kigyō-hōshin 企業方針
distribution policy ryūtsū-seisaku 流通政策
divided policy haitō-seisaku 配当政策
investment policy tōshi-hōshin 投資方針
personnel policy jinji-hōshin 人事方針
pricing policy kakaku-kettei-hōshin 価格決定方針
promotional policy shōshin-seisaku 昇進政策
remittance policy sōkin-hōhō 送金方法
sales policy hanbai-seisaku 販売政策
selling policy hanbai-seisaku 販売政策
wage policy chingin-seisaku 賃金政策
policy execution hōshin no jisshi 方針の実施
policy formulation hōshin no kōshikika 方針の公式化
policy statement gyōmu-hōkoku 業務報告
poll tax jintō-zei 人頭税
pooling arrangements ikkatsu-keiyaku 一括契約
portfolio:
asset portfolio shisan-meisaihyō 資産明細表
balanced portfolio kinkō no yoi shisan-naiyō 均衡のよい資産内容
brand portfolio yūka-shōken-ichiranhyō 有価証券一覧表
business portfolio eigyō-meisaihyō 営業明細表
product portfolio seihin-meisaihyō 製品明細表
stock portfolio yūka-shōken-ichiranhyō 有価証券一覧表
portfolio management shisan-kanri 資産管理
portfolio selection shisan-sentaku 資産選択
position:
competitive position kyōsōteki-shisei 競争的姿勢
financial position zaimu-jōtai 財務状態
positioning taido-chōsei 態度調整
positive discrimination sekkyokuteki-sabetsu 積極的差別
post-entry closed shop kurōzudo-shoppu ni tsuika-kanyū-suru クローズドショップに追加加入する
post-industrialization datsu-kōgyōka 脱工業化
potential:
development potential hatten-senzairyoku 発展潜在力
growth potential senzai-seichōryoku 潜在成長力
management potential keieisha no senzai-nōryoku 経営者の潜在能力
market potential shijō-senzairyoku 市場潜在力
sales potential hanbai-

kanōsei 販売可能性
potential buyer senzaiteki-kaite 潜在的買い手
power:
earning power shūekiryoku 収益力
PPBS (planning, programming, budgeting system) kikaku-keikaku-yosan-hōshiki 企画計画予算方式
PR (public relations) kōhō-katsudō 公報活動
practices:
management practices keiei-kankō 経営慣行
restrictive practices torihiki-seigen 取引制限
predator ryakudatsusha 略奪者
predetermined motion time system (PMTS) yotei-dōsa-jikan-hōshiki 予定動作時間方式
pre-emptive bid shinkabu-hikiukeken-nyūsatsu 新株引受権入札
premium tesūryō 手数料
premium bonus dekidaka-warimashi-teate 出来高割増手当て
present value method gen-kahō 現価法
president shachō 社長
vice-president fuku-shachō 副社長
pressure atsuryoku 圧力
prestige pricing meisei-kakaku 名声価格
preventive maintenance teikiteki-hoshu 定期的保守
price *v.* kakaku o kimeru 価格を決める
price:
competitive price kyōsōteki-kakaku 競争的価格
cut prices *v.* nebiki-suru 値引きする
differential price sabetsu-teki-kakaku 差別的価格
market price shijō-kakaku 市場価格
resale price maintenance (RPM) saihan-kakaku-iji (-seido) 再販価格維持（制度）
spot price genbutsu-kakaku 現物価格
price-cutting kakaku-kirisage 価格切り下げ
price determination kakaku-kettei 価格決定
price differential kakaku-kakusa 価格格差
price discrimination kakaku-sabetsu 価格差別
price-earnings ratio (P/E) kabuka-shūekiritsu 株価収益率
price escalation kakaku-jōshō 価格上昇
price factor kakaku-kettei-yōin 価格決定要因
non price factor hi-kakaku-kettei-yōin 非価格決定要因
price-fixing kakaku-kyōtei 価格協定
price follower kakaku-tsuizui-sha 価格追随者
price index kakaku-shisū 価格指数
retail price index (RPI) kouri-kakaku-shisū 小売り価格指数
price leader medama-shōhin 目玉商品
price range nehaba 値幅

price-sensitive information kakaku o sayū-suru jōhō 価格を左右する情報
price structure kakaku-kōsei 価格構成
pricing kakaku-kettei 価格決定
differential pricing sabetsu-teki-kakaku-seido 差別的価格制度
marginal pricing genkai-kakaku (-kettei) 限界価格(決定)
penetration pricing shijō-shintō-kakaku (-settei) 市場浸透価格（設定）
psychological pricing shinriteki-kakaku (-settei) 心理的価格（設定）
target pricing mokuhyō-kakaku 目標価格
pricing policy kakaku-kettei-hōshin 価格決定方針
pricing strategy kakaku-kettei-senryaku 価格決定戦略
primary commodity dai-ichiji-sanpin 第一次産品
priming:
pump priming yobimizu-seisaku 呼び水政策
print out *v.* insatsu-suru 印刷する
printout insatsu-shutsuryoku 印刷出力
prioritize *v.* yūsenken o ataeru 優先権を与える
privatization min'eika 民営化
privatize *v.* min'eika-suru 民営化する
pro rata hirei-shite 比例して
proactive junkō no 順向の
proactive strategy senken-yūsen-senryaku 先験優先戦略
probability theory kakuritsu-riron 確率理論
problem analysis mondai-bunseki 問題分析
problem area mondai-ryōiki 問題領域
problem solving mondai-kai-ketsu 問題解決
procedure tetsuzuki 手続き
administrative control procedure keiei-kanri-tetsuzuki 経営管理手続き
grievance procedure kujō-shori (-tetsuzuki) 苦情処理(手続き)
procedures:
systems and procedures seido oyobi tetsuzuki 制度および手続き
procedural tetsuzuki-jō no 手続き上の
process *v.* kakō-suru 加工する
process:
decision process ishi-kettei-purosesu 意志決定プロセス
flow process chart nagare-sagyō-kōteizu 流れ作業工程図
interactive process kuri-kaeshi-sagyō 繰り返し作業
logistic process kōhō-shi-en (-tetsuzuki) 後方支援（手続き）
production process seisan-kōtei 生産工程
process control kōtei-kanri 工程管理
process costing kōtei-betsu-genka-keisan 工程別原価計算
process equipment layout

seisan-kōtei-shisetsu no haichi 生産工程施設の配置
processing:
automatic data processing (ADP) jidō-dētā-shorihō 自動データー処理法
batch processing ikkatsu-shori 一括処理
central processing unit (CPU) chūō-shori-sōchi 中央処理装置
data processing dētā-shori データー処理
electronic data processing (EDP) denshi(shiki)-jōhō-shori 電子（式）情報処理
information processing jōhō-shori 情報処理
processor:
word processor (WP) wāpuro ワープロ
procurement chōtatsu 調達
product:
by-product fuku-sanbutsu 副産物
new-product development shinseihin-kaihatsu 新製品開発
pioneer product senkuteki-seihin 先駆的製品
product abandonment seisan-chūshi 生産中止
product advertising seihin-kōkoku 製品広告
product analysis seihin-bunseki 製品分析
product area seihin-han'i 製品範囲
product conception seihin-gainen 製品概念
product costing kobetsu-genka-keisan 個別原価計算
product design seihin-sekkei 製品設計
product development seihin-kaihatsu 製品開発
product differentiate *v.* seihin o sabetsuka-suru 製品を差別化する
product differentiation seihin-sabetsuka 製品差別化
product diversification seihin-tayōka 製品多様化
product dynamics seisan-rikigaku 生産力学
product group seihin-gurūpu 製品グループ
product image seihin-imēji 製品イメージ
product improvement seihin-kaizen 製品改善
product launch shinseihin no uridashi 新製品の売り出し
product life seihin-jumyō 製品寿命
product life cycle seihin-jumyō 製品寿命
product management seihin-kanri 製品管理
product manager seihin-kanrisha 製品管理者
product mix seihin-kōsei 製品構成
product performance seihin-seinō 製品性能
product planning seihin-keikaku 製品計画
product portfolio seihin-meisaihyō 製品明細表
product profile seihin-shōkai 製品紹介
product range seihin-bun'ya 製品分野
product reliability seihin-shinraisei 製品信頼性

product research seihin-chōsa 製品調査
product strategy seihin-senryaku 製品戦略
product testing seihin-kensa 製品検査
product value:
maximum product value saidai-seihin-kachi 最大製品価値
production:
batch production ikkatsu-seisan 一括生産
continuous-flow production renzoku-nagare-sagyō-seisan 連続流れ作業生産
flow production nagare-seisan 流れ生産
intensive production shū-chū-seisan 集中生産
straight production cho-kusen-seisan 直線生産
mass production tairyō-seisan 大量生産
modular production mo-jurā-seisan モジュラー生産
pilot production shisaku 試作
share of production plan seisan-keikaku no buntan 生産計画の分担
production control seisan-kanri 生産管理
production costs seisanhi 生産費
production engineering sei-san-kōgaku 生産工学
production management seisan-kanri 生産管理
production manager seisan-kanrisha 生産管理者
production planning seisan-keikaku 生産計画
production planning and control seisan-keikaku- kanri 生産計画管理
production process seisan-kōtei 生産工程
production run keiyakuryō 契約量
production schedule seisan-keikaku 生産計画
production standard seisan-kijun 生産基準
production target seisan-mokuhyō 生産目標
productive maintenance seisanteki-setsubi-hozen 生産的設備保全
productivity seisansei 生産性
productivity arrangement seisansei-kōjō-kyōtei 生産性向上協定
productivity bargaining seisansei-kōshō 生産性交渉
productivity campaign seisansei-kōjō-undō 生産性向上運動
productivity drive seisansei-kōjō-undō 生産性向上運動
productivity measurement seisansei-sokutei 生産性測定
professionalization senmonka-yōsei 専門家養成
profile:
acquisition profile shutoku-seiseki 取得成績
company profile kigyō-gaiyō 企業概要
customer profile kokyaku-gaiyō 顧客概要
job profile shokumu-setsumei 職務説明
market profile shijō-purofīru

市場プロフィール
risk profile kiken-purofīru 危険プロフィール
profit rieki 利益
cost-volume-profit analysis son'eki-bunseki 損益分析
gross profit sōrijun 総利潤
net profit jun'eki 純益
retained profit ryūho-rijun 留保利潤
profit centre rieki-tan'i-bumon 利益単位部門
profit centre accounting rieki-tan'i-bumon-kaikei 利益単位部門会計
profit-factor analysis rieki-yōin-bunseki 利益要因分析
profit goal rieki-mokuhyō 利益目標
profit impact rieki-kōka 利益効果
profit implication rijun-renrui 利潤連類
profit improvement rieki-kaizen 利益改善
profit margin shōkokin 証拠金
profit maximization rieki-kyokudaika 利益極大化
profit motive rijun-dōki 利潤動機
profit optimization rijun-saitekika 利潤最適化
profit outlook rieki-mitōshi 利益見通し
profit planning rijun-keikaku 利潤計画
profit projection rijun-keikaku 利潤計画
profit-related pay rijun-bunpai-kyūyo 利潤分配給与
profit-sharing rieki-haibun 利益配分
profit strategy rieki-senryaku 利益戦略
profit target rieki-mokuhyō 利益目標
profit-volume ratio (P/V) uriagedaka-genkai-riekiritsu 売上高限界利益率
profitability shūekisei 収益性
profitability analysis shūekisei-bunseki 収益性分析
profits tax rijunzei 利潤税
program *v.* puroguramu o sakusei-suru プログラムを作製する
computer program konpyūta-puroguramu コンピュータ・プログラム
programme *v.* puroguramu o sakusei-suru プログラムを作製する
programme pruroguramu プログラム
development programme kaihatsu-keikaku 開発計画
investment programme tōshi-puroguramu 投資プログラム
trading programme torihiki-keikaku 取引計画
programme budgeting keikaku-betsu-yosansei 計画別予算性
programme evaluation and review technique (PERT) pattohō パット法
programme package sōgō-puroguramu 総合プログラム
programmed learning puroguramudo-gakushū プログラムド学習
programmed management keikakuteki-keiei-kanri 計画

的経営管理
programmer:
computer programmer konpyūta-purogramā コンピュータ・プログラマー
programming puroguramingu プログラミング
computer programming konpyūta-puroguramingu コンピュータ・プログラミング
dynamic programming dōteki-keikakuhō 動的計画法
linear programming senkei -keikakuhō 線型計画法
mathematical programming sūri-keikakuhō 数理計画法
non-linear programming hisenkei-keikakuhō 非線型計画法
parametric programming parametarikku-keisan パラメタリック計算
scientific programming kagakuteki-puroguramingu 科学的プログラミング
progress:
work in progress shikake-hin 仕掛け品
progress control kōtei-kanri 工程管理
progression:
salary progression curve kyūyo-ruishin-kyokusen 給与累進曲線
project:
capital project evaluation shihon-keikaku-hyōka 資本計画評価
chunk a project *v.* pro-jekuto o tsubusu プロジェクトをつぶす
project analysis purojekuto-bunseki プロジェクト分析
project assessment pro-jekuto-hyōka プロジェクト評価
project management puro-jekuto-kanri プロジェクト管理
integrated project management (IPM) sōgō-keikaku-kanri 総合計画管理
project manager purojekuto-manējā プロジェクト・マネージャー
project planning kobetsu-kei-kaku 個別計画
promotion:
promotion (personnel) shōshin 昇進
sales promotion hanbai-sokushin 販売促進
promotional shōshin no 昇進の
promotional mix hanbai-soku-shin-sōgō-shudan 販売促進総合手段
promotional policy hanbai-sokushin-seisaku 販売促進政策
proposal:
business proposal gyōmu-teian 業務提案
value proposal hyōkagaku-teian 評価額提案
proposition:
unique selling proposition (USP) sabetsu-tokusei 差別特性
prospects:
market prospects shijō-tenbō 市場展望
protection:

consumer protection shōhisha-hogo 消費者保護
data protection dētā-hogo データー保護
turf protection shōken-hogo 商権保護

provision:
open network provision kaihōshiki-tsīshinmō-setsubi 開放式通信網設備

PSBR (public sector borrowing requirement) kōkyō-bumon-shakuyō-jōken 公共部門借用条件

PSDR (public sector debt repayment) kōkyō-bumon-fusai-hensai 公共部門負債返済

psychological pricing shinri-teki-kakaku (-settei) 心理的価格（設定）

psychology:
industrial psychology sangyō-shinrigaku 産業心理学

psychometric testing shinri-shiken 心理試験

public:
go public *v.* kabushiki o kōbo-suru 株式を公募する

public enterprise kōei-kigyō 公営企業

public relations (PR) kōhō-katsudō 公報活動

public sector borrowing requirement (PSBR) kōkyō-bumon-kariirekin-jōken 公共部門借入金条件

public sector debt repayment kōkyō-bumon-fusai-hensai-jōken 公共部門負債返済条件

public utility kōkyō-jigyō 公共事業

publicly listed company kabushiki-kōkai-kigyō 株式公開企業

publishing:
desktop publishing takujō-shuppan 卓上出版

pump priming yobi-mizu (seisaku) 呼び水（政策）

purchaser tokuisaki 得意先

purchasing kōnyī 購入

purchasing manager shiire-buchō 仕入部長

purchasing power kōbairyoku 購買力

put out-house *v.* gaichī-suru 外注する

P/V (profit-volume ratio) uriagedaka-genkai-riekiritsu 売上高限界利益率

Q

QC (quality control) hin-shitsu-kanri 品質管理
total QC tōgōteki-hinshitsu-kanri 統合的品質管理
quality assessment hinshitsu-hyōka 品質評価
quality assurance hinshitsu-hoshō 品質保証
quality circle hinshitsu-kanri-shō-gurūpu 品質管理小グループ
quality control (QC) hin-shitsu-kanri 品質管理
quality management hin-shitsu-kanri 品質管理
total quality management (TQM) tōgōteki-hinshitsu-kanri 統合的品質管理
quantitative analysis keiryō-bunseki 計量分析
quantity:
break-even quantity son'eki-bunki-ryō 損益分岐量
economic batch quantity batchi-keizairyō バッチ経済量
economic manufacturing quantity saiteki-seisanryō 最適生産量
economic order quantity saiteki-hatchūryō 最適発注量
quarter shihanki 四半期
quarterage shihanki-barai 四半期払い
queueing theory machiawase-riron 待ち合せ理論
quick assets tōza-shisan 当座資産
quick-fire (situation) soku-shahō 速射法
quick fix sokuji-kettei 即時決定
quota:
sales quota hanbai-wariate (-ryō) 販売割当（量）
quotient shōbai 商売

R

R & D (research and development) kenkyū-kaihatsu 研究開発
raid a company *v.* kaisha e teire-suru 会社へ手入れする
raider:
corporate raider nottoriya 乗っ取り屋
raising:
capital raising shikin-chō-tatsu 資金調達
RAM (random-access memory) tōsoku-yobidashi-kioku-sōchi 等速呼び出し記憶装置
random access randamu-akusesu ランダムアクセス
random-access memory (RAM) tōsoku-yobidashi-kioku-sōchi 等速呼び出し記憶装置
random observation method musakui-kansatsuhō 無作為観察法
random sampling mini-chū-shutsuhō ミニ抽出法
range:
price range nehaba 値幅
product range seihin-bunya 製品分野
ranking jun'i 順位
rat race nezumi-kyōsō 鼠競争
rate:
bank rate ginkō-kinri 銀行金利
base rate kihon-ryōkin 基本料金
forward rate sakimono-sōba 先物相場
going rate genkō-kinri 現行金利
real economic growth rate jisshitsu-keizai-seichō-ritsu 実質経済成長率
rate of return shūeki-ritsu 収益率
internal rate of return (IRR) naibu-shūeki-ritsu 内部収益率
rating:
credit rating shin'yō-kaku-zuke 信用格付け
market rating shijō-kaku-zuke 市場格付け
merit rating seiseki-hyōka 成績評価
performance rating tassei-do-satei 達成度査定
personnel rating jinji-kōsa 人事考査
points-rating method tensū-hyōkahō 点数評価法
ratio:
accounting ratio kaikei-hiritsu 会計比率
administration-production ratio keiei-seisan-ritsu 経営生産率
capital-output ratio shihon-keisū 資本係数
cash ratio genkin-hiritsu 現金比率
cover ratio shōkokin-ritsu 証拠金率
current ratio ryūdō-hiritsu 流動比率
debt ratio saimu-hiritsu 債務比率
debt-equity ratio fusai-tai-

shihon-ritsu 負債対資本率
dynamic ratio dōteki-buai 動的歩合
financial ratio zaimu-hiritsu 財務比率
liquidity ratio ryūdōsei-hiritsu 流動性比率
management ratio keiei-hiritsu 経営比率
price-earnings ratio (P/E) kabuka-shūeki-ritsu 株価収益率
profit-volume ratio (P/V) uriagedaka-genkai-rieki-ritsu 売上高限界利益率

rationale rironteki 理論的
rationalization gōrika 合理化
rationing:
capital rationing shihon-busoku 資本不足
re-image *v.* saisenden-suru 再宣伝する
reach a deal *v.* torihiki ga seiritsu-suru 取り引きが成立する
reactive hannō 反応
reactive strategy saikasseika-senryaku 再活性化戦略
read-only memory (ROM) kotei-kioku-sōchi 固定記憶装置
real economic growth rate jisshitsu-keizai-seichō-ritsu 実質経済成長率
real income jisshitsu-shotoku 実質所得
real time riaru-taimu リアルタイム
recognition:
brand recognition shōhyō-ninshikido 商標認識度
mutual recognition sōgo-hyōka 相互評価
reconfiguration saikōchiku 再構築
record:
track record torakku-rekōdo トラック・レコード
recovery:
overhead recovery kan-setsuhi-kaishū 間接費回収
recovery of expenses keihi no kaishū 経費の回収
recruit *v.* shinki-saiyō-suru 新規採用する
recruitment saiyō 採用
recycle *v.* sairiyō-suru 再利用する
recycling sairiyō 再利用
redeploy *v.* saihaichi-suru 再配置する
redeployment saihaibi 再配備
reduction:
cost reduction keihi-sakugen 経費削減
variety reduction shōhin-shurui-seiri 商品種類整理
redundancy jūfuku 重複
registered trademark tōroku-shōhyō 登録商標
regression analysis kaiki-bunseki 回帰分析
multiple regression analysis (MRA) tajū-kaiki-bunseki 多重回帰分析
regulate *v.* kisei-suru 規制する
regulation kisei 規制
reinvent the wheel *v.* kikō o saisei-suru 機構を再生する
relations:
business relations torihiki-kankei 取引関係
employee relations jūgyōin-kankei 従業員関係

external relations taigai-kankei 対外関係
functional relations kinō-kankei 機能関係
human relations ningen-kankei 人間関係
industrial relations rōshi-kankei 労使関係
labour relations rōdō-kankei 労働関係
public relations (PR) kōhō-katsudō 公報活動

reliability shinraido 信頼度

relief:
double taxation relief nijū-kazei-menjo 二重課税免除
tax relief genzei 減税

remittance policy sōkin-hōhō 送金方法

remuneration hōshū 報酬

reorganization saihensei 再編成

replacement costs saishutoku-genka 再取得原価

report:
status report jōkyō-hōkoku 状況報告

representation:
joint representation kyōdō-daihyōken 共同代表権
worker representation rōdōsha-daihyō (sei) 労働者代表（制）

rerun *v.* yarinaoshi-suru やり直しする

resale price saihan-kakaku 再販価格

resale price maintenance (RPM) saihan-kakaku-iji (-seido) 再販価格維持（制度）

research:
advertising research kōkoku-chōsa 広告調査
consumer research shōhi-sha-chōsa 消費者調査
desk research tōkei-chōsa 統計調査
economic research keizai-chōsa 経済調査
field research jitchi-chōsa 実地調査
market research shijō-chōsa 市場調査
marketing research shijō-chōsa 市場調査
motivational research dōki-chōsa 動機調査
operational research (OR) gyōmu-chōsa 業務調査
operations research (OR) gyōmu-chōsa 業務調査
product research seihin-chōsa 製品調査

research and development (R & D) kenkyū-kaihatsu 研究開発

research department kenkyū-kaihatsubu 研究開発部

reserve:
contingency reserve gūhatsu-sonshitsu-hikiatekin 偶発損失引当金

resistance:
consumer resistance shōhisha-teikō 消費者抵抗

resource:
manpower resource jinteki-shigen 人的資源

resource management shigen-kanri 資源管理

resourcing:
staff resourcing shokuin-kyōkyū 職員供給

response:
anticipatory response senkō-ōtō 先行応答
lag response chien-kaitō 遅延回答
responsibilities:
allocation of responsibilities sekinin-buntan 責任分担
responsibility:
functional responsibility kinōteki-sekinin 機能的責任
linear responsibility shokumu-sekinin (sei) 職務責任(制)
responsive:
consumer responsive shōhisha-hannō 消費者反応
restriction:
trade restriction bōeki-kisei 貿易規制
restrictive practices:
(industrial) seigen-kankō 制限慣行
(legal) torihiki-seigen 取引制限
restructure *v.* saihensei-suru 再編成する
restructuring saihensei 再編成
results:
payment by results nōritsukyū 能率給
retail price index (RPI) kouri-kakaku-shisū 小売価格指数
retained earnings shanai-ryūho-riekikin 社内留保利益金
retained profits naibu-ryūho 内部留保
retire *v.* intai-suru 引退する
retirement taishoku 退職
early retirement sōki-teinen 早期定年
retraining saikunren 再訓練
retrieval:
data retrieval dētā-kensaku データー検索
information retrieval jōhō-kensaku 情報検索
return:
fair return tekisei-hōshū 適正報酬
internal rate of return (IRR) naibu-shūeki-ritsu 内部収益率
rate of return shūeki-ritsu 収益率
return on capital shihon-rimawari 資本利回り
return on capital employed (ROCE) shiyō-shihon-kōritsu 使用資本効率
return on equity (ROE) junshisan-kōritsu 純資産効率
return on investment (ROI) tōshi-kōritsu 投資効率
return on sales hanbai-rieki 販売利益
revaluation of assets shisan-saihyōka 資産再評価
revenue:
average revenue heikin-shūnyū 平均収入
revenue expenditure (revex) shūekiteki-shishutsu 収益的支出
revex (revenue expenditure) shūekiteki-shishutsu 収益的支出
review *v.* saikentō-suru 再検討する
review:
financial review zaimu-minaoshi 財務見直し
performance review sagyō-hyōka 作業評価
salary review kyūyo-

minaoshi 給与見直し
revolving credit kaiten-shin'yō-kanjō 回転信用勘定
revolving fund kaiten-shikin 回転資金
rich:
cash-rich yutaka na temoto-ryūdōsei 豊かな手元流動性
rights issue kabunushi-wari-ate-hakkō 株式割り当て発行
ring fence *v.* kakoikomu 囲い込む
risk analysis kiken-bunseki 危険分析
risk assessment kiken-satei 危険査定
risk capital kiken-shihon 危険資本
risk management kiken-kanri 危険管理
risk profile kiken-gaisetsu 危険概説
risk taking kiken-futan 危険負担
risks:
minimize risks *v.* kiken o kyokushōka-suru 危険を極小化する
robot robotto ロボット
robotics robotto-kōgaku ロボット工学
robotize robottoka-suru ロボット化する
robust takumashii たくましい
ROCE (return on capital employed) shiyō-shihon-kōritsu 使用資本効率
ROI (return on investment) tōshi-kōritsu 投資効率
role-playing jitsuen-kunren (-hō) 実演訓練（法）
role set shokumu-ichiran (hyō) 職務一覧（表）
roll out *v.* purosesu o kioku-sōchi kara nozoku プロセスを記憶装置から除く
ROM (read-only memory) kotei-kioku-sōchi 固定記憶装置
rotation:
job rotation haichi-tenkan 配置転換
round:
in round figures gaisū de 概数で
pay round kyūyo-kikan 給与期間
round off *v.* kai no kazu o kirisuteru 下位の数を切り捨てる
route *v.* hassō-suru 発送する
route keiro 経路
diagnostic route shindan-hōhō 診断方法
routine:
diagnostic routine shindan-rūchin 診断ルーチン
routing sagyō-kōtei 作業工程
royalty tokkyo-shiyōryō 特許使用料
RPI (retail price index) kouri-kakaku-shisū 小売価格指数
RPM (resale price maintenance) saihan-kakaku-iji 再販価格維持
running expenses kōtei-keikaku-hiyō 工程計画費用

S

safety:
margin of safety anzen-yoyūritsu 安全余裕率
safety bank anzen-ginkō 安全銀行
safety management anzen-kanri 安全管理
safety stock anzen-zaiko 安全在庫
salary grade kyūyo-tōkyū 給与等級
salary progression curve kyūyo-ruishin-kyokusen 給与累進曲線
salary review kyūyo-minaoshi 給与見直し
salary structure kyūyo-kōzō 給与構造
sales:
break-even sales saisan-hanbai (ryō) 採算販売（量）
impulse sales hanbai-sokushin 販売促進
return on sales hanbai-shūeki-ritsu 販売収益率
sales analysis uriage-bunseki 売上分析
sales appeal hanbai-sokyū 販売訴求
sales area hanbai-chiiki 販売地域
sales budget hanbai-yosan 販売予算
sales coverage sērusu-kaba-rejji セールスカバレッジ
sales department eigyōbu 営業部
sales drive hanbai-kakuchō-undō 販売拡張運動
sales estimate uriage-mitsumori 売上見積
sales expansion effort hanbai-kakuchō-doryoku 販売拡張努力
sales expectations uriage-kitai 売上期待
sales force hanbairyoku 販売力
sales forecast hanbai-mitsumori 販売見積
sales goal hanbai-mokuhyō 販売目標
sales management hanbai-kanri 販売管理
sales manager hanbai-sekininsha 販売責任者
sales mix uriagehin-kōsei 売上品構成
sales network hanbaimō 販売網
sales planning hanbai-keikaku 販売計画
sales policy hanbai-seisaku 販売政策
sales potential hanbai-kanōsei 販売可能性
sales promotion hanbai-soku-shin (saku) 販売促進（策）
sales quota hanbai-wariate (-ryō) 販売割当（量）
sales talk shōdan 商談
sales territory hanbai-kuiki 販売区域
sales turnover hanbai-kaiten-ritsu 販売回転率
sales volume hanbairyō 販売量
sampling:
activity sampling gyōmu-mihon 業務見本

random sampling nin'i-chūshutsuhō 任意抽出法
statistical sampling tōkeiteki-hyōhon-chūshutsu 統計的標本抽出

satisfaction:
consumer satisfaction shōhisha-manzoku 消費者満足
job satisfaction shokumu no manzokudo 職務の満足度

satisfy *v.* hensai-suru 返済する

saturation:
market saturation shijō-shintō 市場浸透

scab suto-yaburi スト破り

scale:
diseconomy of scale kibo no fukeizaisei 規模の不経済性
economy of scale kibo no keizaisei 規模の経済性
sliding scale suraido-sei スライド制

scan:
environmental scan kankyō-chōsa 環境調査

scanning yōten-haaku 要点把握

scatter diagram sanpuzu 散布図

scenario kyakuhon 脚本
best-case scenario saizen no shinario 最善のシナリオ
worst-case scenario saiaku no shinario 最悪のシナリオ

schedule *v.* yotei o tateru 予定を立てる

schedule yotei (hyō) 予定(表)
production schedule seisan-keikaku 生産計画

scheduling yotei (-sakusei) 予定（作成）
production scheduling seisan-keikaku 生産計画

scheme:
bonus scheme shōyo-seido 賞与制度
incentive scheme shōrei-seido 奨励制度
suggestion scheme teian-seido 提案制度

science:
behavioural science kōdō-kagaku 行動科学
management science keiei-kagaku 経営科学

scientific management kagakuteki-kanri (hō) 科学的管理（法）

scientific programming kagakuteki-puroguramingu 科学的プログラミング

screen *v.* shikaku-shisa-suru 視覚示唆する

screwdriver factory tanjun-sagyō-kōjō 単純作業工場

search:
executive search kanrishoku-saiyō (-jigyō) 管理職採用（事業）

second guess *v.* yosō-suru 予想する

second guessing yosō 予想

securities yūka-shōken 有価証券

securitization shōkenka 証券化

securitize *v.* shōkenka-suru 証券化する

security:
collateral security tanpo-shōken 担保証券
industrial security sangyō-

himitsu-hoji (-seido) 産業秘密保持（制度）
job security shokumu-hoshō 職務保証
unlisted security mijōjō-shōken 未上場証券
security audit anzen-kansa 安全監査
security leak himitsu no rōei 秘密の漏洩
seed money motokin 元金
segment *v.* saibunka-suru 細分化する
segmentation saibunka 細分化
market segmentation shijō-saibunka 市場細分化
segments:
market segments shijō-kubun 市場区分
selection:
portfolio selection shisan-sentaku 資産選択
self-actualization jiko-jitsugenka 自己実現化
self-appraisal jiko-hyōka 自己評価
self-financing jiko-kin'yū 自己金融
self-liquidating jiko-kaishū 自己回収
self-motivation jiko-happun 自己発憤
sell:
hard sell gōin na hanbai 強引な販売
soft sell odayaka na shohō 穏やかな商法
sell-by date gentei-kikan-hanbai 限定期間販売
sell out *v.* uritsukusu 売り尽くす
sellers' market urite-shijō 売り手市場
selling:
direct selling chokusetsu-hanbai 直接販売
hard selling gōin na urikata 強引な売り方
soft selling odayaka na urikomi 穏やかな売り込み
switch selling akaji-hanbai 赤字販売
selling policy hanbai-seisaku 販売政策
semiconductor handōtai 半導体
semi-skilled labour han-jukuren (kō) 半熟練（工）
semi-variable costs jun-hendōhi 準変動費
sensitive:
cost-sensitive kakaku-binkansei 価格敏感性
market-sensitive shijō-binkansei 市場敏感性
sensitivity analysis kando-bunseki 感度分析
sensitivity training kanjusei-kunren 感受性訓練
sensitize *v.* sensu o migaku センスを磨く
sequential analysis chikuji-bunseki 逐次分析
series:
time series jikeiretsu 時系列
services:
after-sales service afutā-sābisu アフターサービス
services:
advisory services komon-gyōmu 顧問業務
computer services kon-

pyūta-sābisu コンピュータサービス
computer services bureau konpyūta-keisan-sentā コンピュータ計算センター
extension services kaku-chō-gyōmu 拡張業務
management services kanri-gyōmu 管理業務
severance pay taishokukin 退職金
sexual harassment seiteki-iyagarase 性的いやがらせ
shakeout (industry) chintai (sangyō) 沈滞（産業）
share:
golden share yūryō-kabu 優良株
market share shijō-sen'yū-ritsu 市場占有率
share capital kabushiki-shihon 株式資本
share of production plan seisan-keikaku no buntan 生産計画の分担
share price performance kabushiki-sōba no jisseki 株式相場の実績
shareholding mochikabu 持ち株
shelf-life chozō-jumyō 貯蔵寿命
shift:
day shift nikkin 日勤
night shift yakin 夜勤
shiftwork kōtaisei 交代制
shop:
closed shop kurōzudo-shoppu クローズドショップ
open shop ōpun-shoppu オープンショップ
post-entry closed shop nyūsha-go no kurōzudo-shoppu 入社後のクローズドショップ
shop floor genba 現場
shop steward kōjō-kanbu 工場幹部
short-term planning tanki-keikaku 短期計画
shortfall akaji 赤字
shortlist kōhosha-meibo 候補者名簿
shortlist *v.* meibo ni noseru 名簿に乗せる
shut-down sōgyō-teishi 操業停止
significant igi-bukai 意義深い
simplex method tantaihō 単体法
simplification:
job simplification gyōmu-tanjunka 業務単純化
work simplification gyōmu-kansoka 業務簡素化
simulate *v.* mogi-suru 模擬する
simulation mogi-renshū 模擬練習
computer simulation konpyūta-shimyurēshon コンピュータシミュレーション
simultaneous engineering dōji-shori-gijutsu 同時処理技術
single currency tan'itsu-tsūka 単一通貨
single market tan'itsu-shijō 単一市場
single sourcing tan'itsu-kyōkyūgen 単一供給源
sinking fund gensai-kikin 減債基金
sit-down strike suwarikomi-sutoraiki 座り込みストライキ
skilled labour jukurenkō 熟練工

skills analysis jukurendo-bunseki 熟練度分析
slack fushin 不振
organizational slack soshiki-teki na fushin 組織的な不振
sliding scale suraido-sei スライド制
slim down *v.* fushin-bumon o kirisuteru 不振部門を切り捨てる
slot tōnyūguchi 投入口
slump fushin 不振
slush fund fusei-shikin 不正資金
smart money chōbatsuteki-songai-baishōkin 懲罰的損害賠償金
smoke-stack industry baien-sangyō 媒煙産業
social analysis shakai-bunseki 社会分析
social security costs shakai-hoshōhi 社会保障費
socio-cultural shakai-bunka-teki 社会文化的
socio-economic shakai-keizai (gaku) 社会経済（学）
sociometric dōteki-ningen-kankei-kenkyū 動的人間関係研究
soft landing nanchakuriku 軟着陸
soft sell odayaka na shōhō 穏やかな商法
soft selling odayaka na urikomi 穏やかな売り込み
software sofutouea ソフトウエア
software application kan-sayō-puroguramu-tekiyō-gyōmu 監査用プログラム適用業務
software broker sofutouea-hanbai-gyōsha ソフトウエア販売業者
software engineer sofutouea-enjinia ソフトウエア・エンジニア
software firm sofutouea-gaisha ソフトウエア会社
software package sofutouea-pakkēji ソフトウエア・パッケージ
software system sofutouea-shisutemu ソフトウエア・システム
sole agent sōdairiten 総代理店
solve *v.* kaiketsu-suru 解決する
solving:
problem solving mondai-kaiketsu 問題解決
source and disposition of funds gensen oyobi shito-shikin 源泉および使途資金
sourcing shigen-kyōkyūgen (no kakuho) 資源供給源（の確保）
dual sourcing fukusū-kyōkyūgen 複数供給源
single sourcing tan'itsu-kyōkyūgen 単一供給源
span:
time span of discretion nin'i-jikantai 任意時間帯
span of control kanri-han'i 管理範囲
Spanish practices supeinteki-kanshū スペイン的慣習
spare capacity yobi-seisan-nōryoku 予備生産能力
specification:
job specification shokumu-

meisaisho 職務明細書
personnel specification jūgyōin-shikakusho 従業員資格書
speed sokudo 速度
spellcheck superu-chekku スペルチェック
spending:
consumer spending kojin-shōhi 個人消費
spin-off effect supin-ofu-kōka スピンオフ効果
spirit:
entrepreneurial spirit kigyōka-seishin 企業家精神
sponsorship kōen 後援
spot price genbutsu-kakaku 現物価格
spreadsheet tenkaihyō 展開表
squeeze:
credit squeeze kin'yū-hiki-shime 金融引き締め
staff shain 社員
staff and line kanbu oyobi rain-yōin 幹部およびライン要員
staff appraisal jūgyōin-hyōka 従業員評価
staff assistant sutaffu-ashisutanto スタッフアシスタント
staff audit jūgyōin-kansa 従業員監査
staff commitment jūgyōin-keiyaku 従業員契約
staff forecasting jūgyōin-(saiyō-) yosoku 従業員（採用）予測
staff inspection teiin-satei 定員査定
staff management shokuin-kanri 職員管理
staff mobility shokuin-idō 職員移動
staff organization sutaffu-soshiki スタッフ組織
staff planning jūgyōin-saiyō-keikaku 従業員採用計画
staff resourcing jūgyōin-kyōkyū 従業員供給
staff transfer jinji-idō 人事移動
staffing jūgyōin-haichi 従業員配置
stag nomi-ya ノミ屋
stagflation fukyō-ka no infure 不況下のインフレ
stagger jisa-shukkin 時差出勤
staggered holidays kōtai-kyūjitsu 交代休日
stake tōshi-shikin 投資資金
stand-alone dokuritsu (no) 独立（の）
stand-alone word processor dokuritsu-gata-wāpuro 独立型ワープロ
standard kijun 基準
budget standard yosan-kijun 予算基準
cost standard genka-kijun 原価基準
financial standard zaimu-kijun 財務基準
performance standard sagyō-kijun 作業基準
production standard seisan-kijun 生産基準
standard costs hyōjun-genka 標準原価
standard costing hyōjun-genka keisan 標準原価計算
standard deviation hyōjun-hensa 標準偏差

standard performance hyōjun-sagyō 標準作業
standard time hyōjun-jikan 標準時間
standardization hyōjunka 標準化
standardize *v.* hyōjunka-suru 標準化する
start-up kaigyō 開業
start-up costs kaigyō-hiyō 開業費用
state of the art kōdo-gijutsu-suijun 高度技術水準
statement:
  financial statement zaimu-shohyō 財務諸表
  mission statement gyōmu-meisaihyō 業務明細表
  policy statement nenji-hōkokusho 年次報告書
  vision statement ichiranhyō 一覧表
statistical control tōkeiteki-kanri 統計的管理
statistical sampling tōkeiteki-hyōhon-chūshutsu 統計的標本抽出
status report genkyō-hōko-kusho 現況報告書
stimulus:
  competitive stimulus kyō-sōteki-shigeki 競争的刺激
stock:
  arbitrage stock sayatori-kabu さやとり株
  blue-chip stock yūryō-kabu 優良株
  buffer stock kanshō-zaiko 緩衝在庫
  gilt-edged stock yūryō-kabu 優良株
  safety stock anzen-zaiko 安全在庫
stock control zaiko (hin) -kanri 在庫（品）管理
stock market shōken-shijō 証券市場
stock option plan kabushiki-yūsen-kaitori-sentakuken (-sei-do) 株式優先買取選択権（制度）
stock portfolio yūka-shōken-ichiranhyō 有価証券一覧表
stock turnover zaikohin-kaiten-ritsu 在庫品回転率
stock valuation zaikohin-hyōka 在庫品評価
stockbroker kabushiki-nakagainin 株式仲買人
stockbroking kabushiki-nakagaigyō 株式仲買業
stocktaking zaikohin-shirabe 在庫品調べ
  continuous stocktaking keizokuteki-zaikohin-shirabe 継続的在庫品調べ
storage:
  computer storage konpyūta-kioku-sōchi コンピュータ記憶装置
store kioku 記憶
strategic alliance senryakuteki-dōmei 戦略的同盟
strategic business unit senryakuteki-bijinesu-tan'i 戦略的ビジネス単位
strategic interdependence senryakuteki-sōgo-ison 戦略的相互依存
strategic planning senryaku-teki-keikaku 戦略的計画
strategy senryaku 戦略
  bottom-up strategy iken-

jōshin-senryaku 意見上申戦略
brand strategy burando-senryaku ブランド戦略
business strategy gyōmu-senryaku 業務戦略
competitive strategy kyōsōteki-senryaku 競争的戦略
corporate strategy kigyō-senryaku 企業戦略
defensive strategy bōei-teki-senryaku 防衛的戦略
diversification strategy tayōka-senryaku 多様化戦略
evolve strategy *v.* senryaku o tenkai-suru 戦略を展開する
executive manpower strategy kanbu-shokuin-saiyō-senryaku 幹部職員採用戦略
executive staff strategy kanbu-shokuin-senryaku 幹部職員戦略
expansion strategy kakudai-senryaku 拡大戦略
financial strategy zaimu-senryaku 財務戦略
growth strategy seichō-senryaku 成長戦略
marketing strategy hanbai-senryaku 販売戦略
negotiation strategy kōshō-senryaku 交渉戦略
pricing strategy kakaku-kettei-senryaku 価格決定戦略
proactive strategy senken-yūsen-senryaku 先験優先戦略
product strategy seihin-senryaku 製品戦略
profit strategy rieki-senryaku 利益戦略
reactive strategy fukko-senryaku 復古戦略
survival strategy ikinokori-senryaku 生き残り戦略
top-down strategy jōi-katatsu-senryaku 上意下達戦略
user strategy tai-shiyōsha-senryaku 対使用者戦略

strategy formulation senryaku-keisei 戦略形成

strategy implementation senryaku-jisshi 戦略実施

stream:
business stream keiei-senryaku 経営戦略
on stream seisan-chū 生産中

streamline *v.* kōritsuka-suru 効率化する

stress:
work stress shigoto no sutoresu 仕事のストレス

stretch break kinchō o yawarageru kyūka 緊張を和らげる休暇

stretching:
brand stretching hinshu-kakudai 品種拡大

strike *v.* sutoraiki o suru ストライキをする

strike:
official strike kōshikiteki-sutoraiki 公式的ストライキ
sit-down strike suwarikomi-sutoraiki 座り込みストライキ
sympathy strike dōjō-suto 同情スト
unofficial strike hikōshiki-sutoraiki 非公式ストライキ
wildcat strike yamaneko-

suto (raiki) 山猫スト（ライキ）

structure *v.* kōsei-suru 構成する

authority structure kenryoku-kōzō 権力構造

capital structure shihon-kōsei 資本構成

corporate structure kigyō-kōsei 企業構成

cost structure genka-kōsei 原価構成

grid structure kōshi-kōzō 格子構造

managerial structure kanri-kikō 管理機構

market structure shijō-kōzō 市場構造

organization structure soshiki-kōsei 組織構成

price structure kakaku-kōsei 価格構成

salary structure kyūyo-kōzō 給与構造

wage structure chingin-kōsei 賃金構成

structuring:

work structuring sagyō-kōsei 作業構成

study:

case study jirei-kenkyū 事例研究

feasibility study junbi-chōsa 準備調査

gap study kakusa-kenkyū 格差研究

market study shijō-kenkyū 市場研究

methods study hōhō-kenkyū 方法研究

motion study dōsa-kenkyū 動作研究

plant layout study seisan-shisetsu-haichi-kenkyū 生産施設配置研究

time and methods study jikan oyobi hōhō-kenkyū 時間および方法研究

time and motion study jikan oyobi dōsa-kenkyū 時間および動作研究

time study jikan-kenkyū 時間研究

work study sagyō-kenkyū 作業研究

style:

house style kigyō no hōshiki 企業の方式

management style kanri-hōshiki 管理方式

sub-optimization bubun-saitekika 部分最適化

subcontract *v.* shitauke-keiyaku o suru 下請け契約をする

subcontractor shitauke-gyōsha 下請け業者

subliminal advertising sen-zai-ishiki-kōkoku 潜在意識広告

subsidiarity hojoteki-gyōmu 補助的業務

subsidiary company kogai-sha 子会社

succession:

management succession planning keiei-keishō-keikaku 経営継承計画

suggestion scheme teian-seido 提案制度

sunrise industry hinode-sangyō 日の出産業

sunset industry shayō-sangyō

斜陽産業
supervise *v.* kantoku-suru 監督する
supervisor kanrisha 管理者
supervisory management kanshi-kanri 監視管理
support activities shien-katsudō 支援活動
supportive shiji (no) 支持（の）
survey:
attitude survey taido-chōsa 態度調査
market survey shijō-chōsa 市場調査
survival strategy ikinokori-senryaku 生き残り戦略
sustainability iji-nōryoku 維持能力
swap:
forward swap dōji-tōgaku-baibai 同時等額売買
SWOT (strengths, weaknesses, opportunities & threats) analysis chōsho, tansho, kikai-atsukai-bunseki 長所短所機会扱分析
switch selling akaji-torihiki 赤字取引
switch trading suitchi-torēdingu スイッチトレーディング
sympathy strike dōjō-suto 同情スト
symposium shinpojiumu シンポジウム
syndicate kigyō-gōdō 企業合同
synergism sōgo-fujo 相互扶助
synergy kyōdō-sagyō 共同作業
system shisutemu システム
business system keiei-soshiki 経営組織
computerized information system (COINS) konpyūta-riyō-jōhō-shisutemu コンピュータ利用情報システム
estimating systems costs shisutemu-genka-mitsumori システム原価見積
expert system senmonka-keiei-shisutemu 専門家経営システム
information system jōhō-shisutemu 情報システム
integrated management system tōgōteki-keiei-jōhō-kanri-seido 統合的経営情報管理制度
management information system (MIS) keiei-jōhō-shisutemu 経営情報システム
planning, programming, budgeting system (PPBS) kikaku-keikaku-yosan-hōshiki 企画計画予算方式
predetermined motion time system (PMTS) yotei-dōsa-jikan-hōshiki 予定動作時間方式
software system sofutoouea-shisutemu ソフトウエアシステム
wage system chingin-seido 賃金制度
systematize *v.* soshikika-suru 組織化する
systematized shisutemuka-shita システム化した
systems analysis shisutemu-bunseki システム分析
systems and procedures seido oyobi tetsuzuki 制度および手続き
systems approach shisutemu-apurōchi システムアプローチ

systems design shisutemu-sekkei システム設計
systems engineering shisutemu-kōgaku システム工学
systems management shisutemu-kanri システム管理
systems planning shisutemu-keikaku システム計画
systems theory shisutemu-riron システム理論

T

TA (transactional analysis) gyōmu-shori-bunseki 業務処理分析
tactical plan senjutsuteki-kun-ren (-keikaku) 戦術的訓練（計画）
tactics:
competitive tactics kyōsō-teki-senjutsu 競争的戦術
take-home pay tedori-kyūryō 手取り給料
take-off ririku 離陸
take-over nottori 乗っ取り
take-over bid (TOB) kabu-shiki-kōkai-kaitsuke 株式公開買い付け
talk:
sales talk shōdan 商談
talks:
pay talks chingin-kōshō 賃金交渉
tangible assets yūkei-shisan 有形資産
target *v.* mokuhyō o settei-suru 目標を設定する
target mokuhyō 目標
production target seisan-mokuhyō 生産目標
profit target rieki-mokuhyō 利益目標
target pricing mokuhyō-kakaku-settei 目標価格設定
target-setting mokuhyō-settei 目標設定
targeting mokuhyō-settei 目標設定
tariff barrier kanzei-shōheki 関税障壁
non-tariff barrier (NTB) hikanzei-shōheki 非関税障壁
task force purojekuto-chīmu プロジェクトチーム
tax *v.* kazei-suru 課税する
tax:
corporation tax hōjin-zei 法人税
income tax shotoku-zei 所得税
payroll tax kyūyo-zei 給与税
poll tax jintō-zei 人頭税
profits tax rijun-zei 利潤税
value added tax (VAT) fuka-kachi-zei 付加価値税
tax-deductible kazei-kōjo 課税控除
tax incentive zeisei-jō no yūgū-sochi 税制上の優遇措置
tax relief genzei 減税
taxation relief:
double taxation relief nijū-kazei-menjo 二重課税免除
team-building shōshūdan-zukuri 小集団作り
team leader chīmu-rīdā チームリーダー
team player chīmu-purēyā チームプレーヤー
tech:
high-tech haiteku ハイテク
low-tech teigijutsu 低技術
techniques:
management techniques keiei-gijutsu 経営技術
technological forecasting gijutsu-yosō 技術予想

technology:
information technology jōhō-gijutsu 情報技術
technology transfer gijutsu-iten 技術移転
teleconference denwa-kaigi 電話会議
telemarketing denwa-torihiki 電話取り引き
telesales denwa ni yoru hanbai 電話による販売
teletext eizō de mirareru teki-suto 映像でみられるテキスト
tender *v.* uridasu 売り出す
tender hanbai-mōshikomi 販売申込
tendering:
competitive tendering kyōsō-nyūsatsu 競争入札
terminal tanmatsu (sōchi) 端末（装置）
computer terminal konpyūta-tanmatsu コンピュータ端末
territory:
sales territory hanbai-kuiki 販売区域
test:
aptitude test tekisei-shiken 適性試験
market test shijō-kensa 市場検査
test marketing shiken-hanbai 試験販売
test run shiunten 試運転
testing:
field testing jitchi-shiken 実地試験
product testing seihin-kensa 製品検査
psychometric testing shinri-shiken 心理試験
T-group training tī-gurūpu-kunren Tグループ訓練
theme:
advertising theme senden-shudai 宣伝主題
theory:
administrative theory keiei-kanri-riron 経営管理理論
communications theory tsūshin-riron 通信理論
contingency theory gū-hatsu-riron 偶発理論
decision theory ishi-kettei-riron 意志決定理論
game theory gēmu no riron ゲームの理論
information theory jōhō-riron 情報理論
management theory keiei-kanri-riron 経営管理理論
organization theory soshiki-ron 組織論
probability theory kaku-ritsu-riron 確率理論
queueing theory machi-awase-riron 待ち合わせ理論
systems theory shisutemu-riron システム理論
think-tank shinku-tanku シンクタンク
think the unthinkable *v.* arisō mo nai koto o kangaeru ありそうもないことを考える
thinking:
creative thinking sōzōteki-shikō 創造的思考
lateral thinking suihei-shikō 水平思考
third country daisan-goku 第三国
third generation daisan-sedai

第三世代
third party daisan-sha 第三者
throughput shori-nōryoku 処理能力
throw money at problems *v.* mondai-kaiketsu ni tsuika-shishutsu-suru 問題解決に追加支出する
thrust:
competitive thrust kyōsō-teki-kōgeki 競争的攻撃
time:
delivery time nōki 納期
down time kyūshi-jikan 休止時間
lead time junbi-jikan 準備時間
predetermined motion time system (PMTS) yotei-dōsa-jikan-hōshiki 予定動作時間方式
real time riaru-taimu リアルタイム
standard time hyōjun-jikan 標準時間
turnaround time tān-ara-undo-taimu ターンアラウンドタイム
time and methods study jikan oyobi hōhō-kenkyū 時間および方法研究
time and motion study jikan oyobi dōsa-kenkyū 時間および動作研究
time frame jikan-kōsei 時間構成
time management jikan-kanri 時間管理
time series jikeiretsu 時系列
time-sharing jibunkatsu (-shori) 時分割（処理）
time sheet kinmu-jikan-kiroku-hyō 勤務時間記録表
time span of discretion nin'i-jikantai 任意時間帯
time study jikan-kenkyū 時間研究
time-lag jikan no zure 時間のずれ
time-phase jisō 時相
toolbox kōgubako 工具箱
top-down jōi-katatsu-hōshiki 上意下達方式
top-down strategy kakō-gata-senryaku 下降型戦略
top management saikō-keiei-sha 最高経営者
top management approach saikō-keiei-sekininsha-seido 最高経営責任者制度
top up *v.* jūbun hokyū-suru 十分補給する
total plant maintenance zen-seisan-kōtei no hoshu 全生産工程の保守
total quality sōgōteki-hinshitsu 総合的品質
total quality control (TQC) tōgō-hinshitsu-kanri 統合品質管理
total quality management (TQM) tōgōteki-hinshitsu-kanri 統合的品質管理
TQM (total quality management) tōgōteki-hinshitsu-kanri 統合的品質管理
trade association sangyō-dantai 産業団体
trade imbalance bōeki-fukinkō 貿易不均衡
trade record sen-kiroku 線記録
trade restriction bōeki-seigen 貿易制限

trade off *v.* uriharau 売り払う
trade-off kōkan 交換
trade union rōdō-kumiai (shokushu-betsu no) 労働組合（職種別の）
traded option baikyaku-zumi no opushon 売却済みのオプション
trademark:
registered trademark tōroku-shōhyō 登録商標
trader bōeki-gyōsha 貿易業者
trading:
insider trading insaidā-torihiki インサイダー取り引き
patent trading tokkyo-baibai 特許売買
switch trading suitchi-torēdingu スイッチトレーディング
trading area torihiki-chiiki 取り引き地域
trading programme torihiki-keikaku 取り引き計画
trainee turnover kunrensei-kaiten-ritsu 訓練生回転率
training kunren 訓練
analytical training bunseki-kunren 分析訓練
booster training saikunren 再訓練
group training dantai-kunren 団体訓練
in-plant training kōjōnai-kunren 工場内訓練
multimedia training maruchimedia- kunren マルチメディア訓練
off-the-job training shokubagai-kunren 職場外訓練
part-analysis training kobetsu-bunseki-kunren 個別分析訓練
sensitivity training kanjusei-kunren 感受性訓練
T-group training tī-gurūpu-kunren Tグループ訓練
vocational training shokugyō-kunren 職業訓練
training needs analysis kunren-nīzu-bunseki 訓練ニーズ分析
training officer kunren-tantōsha 訓練担当者
training within industry (TWI) shokubanai-kunren 職場内訓練
transactional torihiki-jō no 取引上の
transactional analysis (TA) torihiki-bunseki 取り引き分析
transfer:
staff transfer jinji-idō 人事移動
technology transfer gijutsu-iten 技術移転
transfer pricing furikae-kakaku 振替価格
transitional katokiteki 過渡期的
translation (foreign exchange) kansan (gaku) 換算（額）
transportation un'yu 運輸
tree:
decision tree ishi-kettei no keitōzu 意志決定の系統図
family tree keizu 系図
pertinence tree soshikinai-keitōzu 組織内系統図
trend dōkō 動向
economic trend keizai-dōkō 経済動向
exponential trend shisū-

dōkō 指数動向
market trend shijō-dōkō 市場動向
trickle-down theory tori-kkuru-daun-riron トリックル・ダウン理論
troubleshooter funsō-chōtei-nin 紛争調停人
troubleshooting koshō-hakken-shūri 故障発見修理
turf protection shōken-hogo 商圏保護
turn around *v.* motodōri ni modosu 元どおりに戻す
turnaround time tān-araundo-taimu ターンアラウンドタイム
turnover:
inventory turnover zaiko-kaiten-ritsu 在庫回転率
labour turnover rōdō-kaiten-ritsu 労働回転率
sales turnover hanbai-kaiten-ritsu 販売回転率
stock turnover zaikohin no kaiten-ritsu 在庫品の回転率
trainee turnover kunrensei kaiten-ritsu 訓練生回転率
TWI (training within industry) kigyōnai-kunren 企業内訓練

U

unbundle *v.* koko ni kakaku o tsukeru 個々に価格を付ける
unbundling kakaku-bunri 価格分離
unbundling (a business) bunri-keiei 分離経営
undercapacity fusoku-seisan-nōryoku 不足生産能力
undercapitalized shihon-busoku 資本不足
undercut kirisage 切り下げ
undermanned jin'in-busoku no 人員不足の
undermanning jin'in-busoku 人員不足
underperform kashō-sōgyō 過小操業
underprice *v.* kakaku o sageru 価格を下げる
understaffed jūgyōin-busoku no 従業員不足の
understaffing jūgyōin-busoku 従業員不足
unfair competition fukōsei-kyōsō 不公正競争
unfair dismissal futō-kaiko 不当解雇
unique selling proposition (USP) sabetsu-tokusei (shōhin no) 差別特性（商品の）
unit labour costs bumon-betsu-rōmuhi 部門別労務費
unlisted company hi-jōjō-kigyō 非上場企業
unlisted security hi-jōjō-kabushiki 非上場株式
unofficial action hi-kōnin-katsudō 非公認活動
unofficial strike hikōshiki-sutoraiki 非公式ストライキ
unscramble *v.* kaidoku-suru 解読する
unskilled labour mijukurenkō 未熟練工
unstructured hitaikeiteki na 非体系的な
up the line jōkyū-shokuin 上級職員
update *v.* kōshin-suru 更新する
update kōshin 更新
up-market jōshō-sōba 上昇相場
upstream kawakami (sangyō) 川上（産業）
upswing ichijirushii zōka 著しい増加
uptime (comp) shiyō-kanō-jikan 使用可能時間
upturn jōshō 上昇
upwardly mobile jōshō-idō 上昇移動
use-by date shiyō-kikan 使用期間
user attitude shiyōsha no taido 使用者の態度
user-friendly kōiteki-shiyōsha 好意的使用者
user strategy tai-shiyōsha-senryaku 対使用者戦略
user-unfriendly hi-kōiteki-shiyōsha 非好意的使用者
USP (unique selling proposition) sabetsu-tokusei 差別特性
utility:
public utility kōkyō-jigyō 公共事業
utilization:
capacity utilization seisan-nōryoku-riyō 生産能力利用

V

VA (value analysis) kachi-bunseki 価値分析
valuation:
stock valuation zaikohin-hyōka 在庫品評価
value kachi 価値
book value bojō-kakaku 簿上価格
break-up value seisan-kachi 生産価値
market value shijō-kachi 市場価値
net present value (NPV) jun-jika 純時価
present value method jika-hōshiki 時価方式
value added fuka-kachi 付加価値
value added tax (VAT) fuka-kachi-zei 付加価値税
value analysis (VA) kachi-bunseki 価値分析
value chain kachi-taikei 価値体系
value concept kachi-gainen 価値概念
value engineering kachi-kōgaku 価値工学
value proposal kakaku-teiji 価格提示
variance kahensei 可変制
cost variance genka-sagaku 原価差額
variance analysis sai-bunseki 再分析
variety reduction hinshu-sakugen 品種削減
VAT (value added tax) fuka-kachi-zei 付加価値税
VDU (visual display unit) hyōji-sōchi 表示装置
venture:
joint venture gōben-kigyō 合弁企業
joint venture company gōben-gaisha 合弁会社
venture capital kiken-futan-shihon 危険負担資本
venture capitalist benchā-bijinesu-shusshisha ベンチャービジネス出資者
venture management kigyō-keiei 企業経営
verbal:
non-verbal communication higengo-komyunikēshon 非言語コミュニケーション
verbal communication gengo-komyunikēshon 言語コミュニケーション
verify *v.* tenken-suru 点検する
vertical integration suichoku-gappei 垂直合併
vested interest kitoku-ken'eki 既得権益
video bideo ビデオ
viewdata kenshō-shiryō 検証資料
viability seisan-nōryoku 生産能力
viable hatten-nōryoku no aru 発展能力のある
vice-chairman fuku-kaichō 副会長
vice-president fuku-shachō 副社長
virus:
computer virus konpyūta-

uirusu コンピュータ・ウイルス
vision shikaku 視覚
vision statement ichiranhyō 一覧表
visual display unit (VDU) hyōji-sōchi 表示装置
vocational guidance shokugyō-shidō 職業指導
vocational training shokugyō-kunren 職業訓練
volume ryō 量
sales volume uriagedaka 売上高

W

wage chingin 賃金
minimum wage saitei-chingin 最低賃金
wage ceiling chingin-saikō-gendo 賃金最高限度
wage differential chingin-kakusa 賃金格差
wage drift kōshō-chinginsa 交渉賃金差
wage freeze chingin-tōketsu 賃金凍結
wage level chingin-suijun 賃金水準
wage policy chingin-seisaku 賃金政策
wage structure chingin-kōzō 賃金構造
wage system chingin-seido 賃金制度
walkout shokuba-hōki 職場放棄
WAN (wide area network) kōiki-nettowāku 広域ネットワーク
warehousing sōko-gyōmu 倉庫業務
wastage:
natural wastage shizen-sonmō 自然損耗
waste:
industrial waste sangyō-haikibutsu 産業廃棄物
wasting assets genmō-shisan 減耗資産
weighted average kajū-heikin 加重平均
weighting kasan-teate 加算手当
well-packaged yoku junbi-sareta よく準備された
wheeling and dealing kenbō-jussū 権謀術数
white-collar (worker) howai-to-karā ホワイトカラー
white goods daidokoro-yō-denki-seihin 台所用電気製品
white knight sukui no kami 救いの神
whiz-kid kiremono 切れ者
wide area network (WAN) kōiki-nettowāku 広域ネットワーク
wildcat strike yamaneko-suto 山猫スト
Winchester disk uinchesutā-disuku ウインチェスターディスク
wind down *v.* jojo ni owara-seru 徐々に終わらせる
wind up *v.* shiageru 仕上げる
winding up kigyō-heisa 企業閉鎖
window-dressing funshoku-teian 粉飾提案
window of opportunity kikai no shudan 機会の手段
word processor (WP) wāpuro ワープロ
stand-alone word processor dokuritsu-gata-wāpuro 独立型ワープロ
work:
clerical work measurement (CWM) jimu-sagyō-sokutei 事務作業測定
work by contract keiyaku no rikō 契約の履行
work content gyōmu-naiyō 業務内容

work cycle shigoto no saikuru 仕事のサイクル
work in progress shikakehin 仕掛け品
work measurement sagyō-sokutei 作業測定
work schedule sagyō-keikaku 作業計画
work simplification sagyō-tanjunka 作業単純化
work stress shigoto no kinchō 仕事の緊張
work structuring sagyō-kōsei 作業構成
work study gyōmu-chōsa 業務調査
work-to-rule junpō-sutoraiki 順法ストライキ
worker buyout jūgyōin no keieiken-kaitori 従業員の経営権買取
worker participation jūgyōin-keiei-sanka 従業員経営参加
worker representation rōdōsha-daihyō 労働者代表
working capital unten-shikin 運転資金
working hours kinmu-jikan 勤務時間
flexible working hours nin'i-kinmu-jikan 任意勤務時間
working party shigoto-nakama 仕事仲間
workload hyōjun-sagyōryō 標準作業量
workplace shokuba 職場
works committee shokuba-iinkai 職場委員会
works council rōshi-kyōgikai 労使協議会
works manager kōjō-kanrisha 工場管理者
workstation sagyō-tanmatsu 作業端末
world-class kokusai-reberu 国際レベル
worst-case scenario saiaku no shinario 最悪のシナリオ
worth:
net worth jiko-shihon 自己資本
WP (word processor) wāpuro ワープロ
write off *v.* chōkeshi ni suru 帳消しにする
WYSIWYG *(What You See Is What You Get)* mita-tōri 見たとおり

X factor fukakutei-yōso 不確定要素

yardstick kijun-shakudo 基準尺度
year:
  base year kijun-nenji 基準年次
  financial year kaikei-nendo 会計年度
yield hōshū 報酬
  average yield heikin-hōshū 平均報酬
  earnings yield shūeki 収益
yuppie yappī ヤッピー

Z

Z chart zetto-zuhyō Z図表
zaitech zaiteku 財テク
zero-base budget yūsen-jun'i o bapponteki ni minaoshite-sakuseishita yosan 優先順位を抜本的に見直して作成した予算
zero defects mukekkan-undō 無欠陥運動
zero-rating zero-hyōka ゼロ評価
zero-sum game zero-samu-gēmu ゼロサムゲーム

JAPANESE-ENGLISH

A

adoon-setsubi アドオン設備 add-on equipment
afutā-sābisu アフターサービス after-sales service
airo o kaishō-suru 隘路を解消する debottleneck *v.*
aitekoku 相手国 host country
akaji 赤字 shortfall
akaji-hanbai 赤字販売 switch selling
akaji-torihiki 赤字取引 switch selling
akaji-zaisei 赤字財政 deficit financing
anarogu-kigō アナログ記号 analog(ue) representation
anarogu-konpyūta アナログコンピュータ analog(ue) computer
anzen-ginkō 安全銀行 safety bank
anzen-hogo-kansa 安全保護監査 security audit
anzen-kanri 安全管理 safety management
anzen-kansa 安全監査 security audit
anzen-yoyūritsu 安全余裕率 margin of safety
anzen-zaiko 安全在庫 safety stock
ara-rieki 粗利益 gross margin
arisō mo nai koto o kangaeru ありそうもないことを考える think the unthinkable *v.*
atomawashi ni suru 後回しにする put on the back burner *v.*
atsuryoku 圧力 pressure

B

bātā-bōeki バーター貿易 barter trade
baien-sangyō 媒煙産業 smoke-stack industry
baikyaku-kijitsu 売却期日 sell-by date
baikyaku-zumi no opushon 売却済みのオプション traded option
baikyaku-zumi no sentaku-ken 売却済の選択権 traded option
baitai 媒体 media
baitai-bunseki 媒体分析 media analysis
baitai-sentaku 媒体選択 media selection
bandoru-sōsa バンドル操作 bundling
batchi-keizairyō バッチ経済量 economic batch quantity
batchi-seigyo バッチ制御 batch control
batchi-seisan バッチ生産 batch production
bazu-wādo バズワード buzz-word
benchā-bijinesu-shusshisha ベンチャービジネス出資者 venture capitalist
benchā-shihon ベンチャー資本 venture capital
bideo ビデオ video
bijinesu-chūshin (no) ビジネス中心（の） business centric
bijinesu-gēmu ビジネスゲーム management game
bijinesu-mitōshi ビジネス見通し business outlook
bijinesu-pōtoforio ビジネスポートフォリオ business portfolio
bijinesu-soshiki ビジネス組織 business system
bishiteki 微視的 micro
bodī-rangēji ボディーランゲージ body language
bogai-shisan 簿外資産 hidden assets
bojō-kakaku 簿上価格 book value
bōeiteki-senryaku 防衛的戦略 defensive strategy
bōeki-fukinkō 貿易不均衡 trade imbalance
bōeki-gyōsha 貿易業者 trader
bōeki-kisei 貿易規制 trade restriction
bōeki-seigen 貿易制限 trade restriction
bōeki-shōheki 貿易障壁 trade barrier
bōkenteki 冒険的 empirical
bōsen-zuhyō 棒線図表 bar chart
bosuton-bokkusu-bunseki ボストンボックス分析 Boston Box analysis
bosuton-konsarutingu-gurūpu no bunseki ボストンコンサルティンググループの分析 BCG (Boston Consulting Group) analysis
bubun-saitekika 部分最適化 sub-optimization
buchō 部長 general manager
bumon-betsu-genka-keisan 部門別原価計算 functional costing

bumon-betsu-hiyō 部門別費用 unit labour cost
bumon-betsu-keikaku 部門別計画 departmental planning
bumon-betsu-rōmuhi 部門別労務費 unit labour cost
bumon-kanri 部門管理 divisional management
bumon-kanrisha 部門管理者 departmental manager
bun'enzu 分円図 pie chart
bunka 文化 culture
bunkai-suru 分解する chunk down *v.*
bunkatsu-suru 分割する fractionalize *v.*
bunkenteki-keiei 分権的経営 decentralized management
bunri-keiei 分離経営 unbundling (a business)
bunsan-bunseki 分散分析 variance analysis
bunsan-kunren 分散訓練 part-analysis training
bunsanka-suru 分散化する decentralize *v.*
bunseki （グループの）分析 analysis (group)
bunseki-kunren 分析訓練 analytical training
buppin-hanbai-jiten 物品販売時点 point-of-sale material
burando ブランド brand
burando ni taisuru chūseishin ブランドに対する忠誠心 brand loyalty
burando ni taisuru ninki ブランドに対する人気 brand acceptance
burando ni taisuru taido ブランドに対する態度 brand positioning
burando-chūjitsudo ブランド忠実度 brand loyalty
burando-imēji ブランドイメージ brand image
burando-kanrisha ブランド管理者 brand manager
burando-manējā ブランドマネージャー brand manager
burando-ninshiki ブランド認識 brand recognition
burando-pōtoforio ブランドポートフォリオ brand portfolio
burando-senryaku ブランド戦略 brand strategy
burein-sutōmingu ブレインストーミング brainstorming
burōkā ブローカー broker
butteki-kanri 物的管理 physical management
butteki-proguramu-kanri 物的プログラム管理 physical programmed management
butteki-ryūtsū-kanri 物的流通管理 physical distribution management
butteki-seisan-kanri 物的生産管理 physical production management
butteki-seisanbutsu-kanri 物的生産物管理 physical product management
butteki-shisan-kanri 物的資産管理 physical portofolio management
byōdō 平等 equality
byōdō-chingin 平等賃金 equal pay
byōdō-koyō-kikai 平等雇用機会 equal employment opportunity
byōdō-kyūyo 平等給与 equal pay

C

chakuriku 着陸 landing
channeru-kantoku チャンネル監督 channel captain
chien 遅延 lag
chien-kaitō 遅延回答 lag response
chien-ōtō 遅延応答 lag response
chiiki-sekininsha 地域責任者 area manager
chiiki-bunkatsuka-suru 地域分割化する compartmentalize *v.*
chiiki-kanrisha 地域管理者 area manager
chīmu-purēyā チームプレーヤー team player
chīmu-rīdā チームリーダー team leader
chīmu-zukuri チーム作り team building
chikuji-bunseki 逐次分析 sequential analysis
chingashi-suru 賃貸しする lease *v.*
chingin 賃金 wage
chingin-igai no kyūfu 賃金以外の給付 fringe benefits
chingin-kakusa 賃金格差 wage differential
chingin-kōjo 賃金控除 payroll deduction
chingin-kōsei 賃金構成 wage structure
chingin-kōshō 賃金交渉 pay talks
chingin-kōzō 賃金構造 wage structure
chingin-meisaihyō 賃金明細表 payroll
chingin-saikō-gendo 賃金最高限度 wage ceiling
chingin-seido 賃金制度 wage system
chingin-seisaku 賃金政策 wage policy
chingin-suijun 賃金水準 wage level
chingin-tōketsu 賃金凍結 wage freeze
chinpuka 陳腐化 obsolescence
chintai 賃貸 lease-lend
chintai mata wa kaitori 賃貸又は買取 lease or buy
chintai (sangyō) 沈滞（産業) shakeout (industry)
chintai-shisetsu 賃貸施設 borrowing facility
chintaishaku 賃貸借 leasing
chippu チップ chip
chokkanteki-kanri 直感的管理 intuitive management
chokketsu 直結 on line
chokusen-seisan 直線生産 line production
chokusetsu-genka (keisan) 直接原価（計算） direct costing
chokusetsu-hanbai 直接販売 direct selling
chokusetsu-kanshō-kanri 直接干渉管理 hands-on operation
chokusetsu-keihi 直接経費 direct expenses
chokusetsu-koyō 直接雇用 direct hire
chokusetsu-koyō-jūgyōin

直接雇用従業員 direct hire employees
chokusetsu-rōdō 直接労働 direct labour
chokusetsu-torihiki 直接取り引き direct marketing
chōbatsuteki-songai-baishōkin 懲罰的損害賠償金 smart money
chōbo-sōsa 帳簿操作 creative accounting
chōkeshi ni suru 帳消しにする write off *v.*
chōki-keikaku 長期計画 long-term planning
chōki-keizai-keikaku 長期経済計画 long range planning
chōki-saika 長期債化 funding
chōki-shiharai-keikaku 長期支払計画 forward planning
chōsei-katsudō 調整活動 coodination
chōsho, tansho, kikai-atsukai-bunseki 長所短所機会扱分析 strengths, weaknesses, opportunities and threats (SWOT) analysis
chōtatsu 調達 procurement
chōtei 調停 conciliation
chōwa-zukuri 調和作り harmonization
chōwa-saseru 調和させる harmonize *v.*
chozō-jumyō 貯蔵寿命 shelf-life
chūkaku-senryaku 中核戦略 core strategy
chūkan-kanrishoku 中間管理職 middle management
chūmon-seisan 注文生産 custom made
chūmon-seisan-shita 注文生産した customized
chūmon-tori ni mawaru 注文取りに回る canvass *v.*
chūō-enzan-shori-sōchi 中央演算処理装置 central processing unit (CPU)
chūōchi 中央値 median
chūsai 仲裁 arbitration, mediation
chūsai-suru 仲裁する mediate *v.*
chūseishin 忠誠心 loyalty

D

dai-ichiji-sanpin 第一次産品 primary commodity
dai-issen-jūgyōin 第一線従業員 front line employees
dai-issen-kantoku 第一線監督 first-line manager
dai-san-goku 第三国 third country
dai-san-sedai 第三世代 third generation
dai-san-sha 第三者 third party
daidokoro-yō-denki-seihin 台所用電器製品 white goods
daidokoro-yōhin-igai no denki-seihin 台所用品以外の電器製品 brown goods
daihyō-suru 代表する delegate *v.*
dairekuto-mēru ダイレクトメール direct mail
dangō 談合 collusion
dankaiteki ni dōnyū-suru 段階的に導入する phase in *v.*
dankaiteki ni haishi-suru 段階的に廃止する phase out *v.*
danryokusei 弾力性 elasticity
danryokusei-yosan 弾力性予算 flexible budget
danryokuteki-kinmu-jikansei 弾力的勤務時間制 flexible working hours
dantai-kōshō 団体交渉 collective bargaining
dantai-kunren 団体訓練 group training
dantai-rōdō-kyōyaku 団体労働協約 collective bargaining agreement
dantai-shōrei (seido) 団体奨励（制度） group incentive
dantai-shōreikyū 団体奨励給 group incentive
dantai-shōyo 団体賞与 group bonus
datsu-kōgyōka 脱工業化 post-industrialization
dētā-banku データーバンク data bank
dētā-bēsu データーベース data base
dētā-dentatsu-sōchi データー伝達装置 modem
dētā-hanbai データー販売 data selling
dētā-hiyō データー費用 data expenses
dētā-hogo データー保護 data protection
dētā-kensaku データー検索 data retrieval
dētā-nagarezu データー流れ図 data flow chart
dētā-shori データー処理 data processing
dētā-shutoku データー取得 data acquisition
dētā-shūshū データー収集 data acquisition
dētā-tsūshin データー通信 data mail
dejitaru デジタル digital
dejitaru-konpyūta デジタルコンピュータ digital computer
dekidaka-barai 出来高払い payment by results, pay as you earn
dekidaka-warimashi-teate 出来高割増手当て premium

bonus
dendō-sōchi 伝動装置 gearing
denshi-dētā-shori 電子データー処理 electronic data processing (EDP)
denshi-shuppan 電子出版 desktop publishing
denshi-shuppan-suru 電子出版する desktop publish *v.*
denshika-sareta-jimusho 電子化された事務所 electronic office
denshi-yūbin 電子郵便 electronic mail (e-mail)
denshishiki-dētā-shori 電子式データー処理 electronic data processing (EDP)
densō-shashin 伝送写真 facsimile
denwa ni yoru hanbai 電話による販売 telesale
denwa-kaigi 電話会議 teleconference
denwa-torihiki 電話取り引き telemarketing
dētā-genka-keisan データー原価計算 data costing
dīrā ディーラー dealer
disuku-doraibu ディスクドライブ disk drive
disuku-kudō-sōchi ディスク駆動装置 disk drive
dokuritsu (no) 独立（の） stand-alone
dokuritsu-gata-wāpuro 独立型ワープロ stand-alone word processor
dokuritsu-saisansei-kaikei 独立採算制会計 profit centre accounting
dokuyaku 毒薬 poison pill
dōgyō-kumiai 同業組合 trade association
dōin-kanō-jin'in 動員可能人員 operations manpower
dōin-kanō-jinteki-shigen-yosoku 動員可能人的資源予測 manpower forecasting
dōji-shori-gijutsu 同時処理技術 simultaneous engineering
dōji-tōgaku-baibai 同時等額売買 forward swap
dōjō-suto 同情スト sympathy strike
dōki 動機 motivation
dōki o ataeru 動機を与える motivate *v.*
dōki o ubau 動機を奪う demotivate *v.*
dōki-chōsa 動機調査 motivational research
dōki-hakai 動機破壊 demotivation
dōki-zuke-suru mono 動機づけするもの motivator
dōkō 動向 trend
dōsa-keizai 動作経済 motion economy
dōsa-kenkyū 動作研究 motion study
dōtai-keiei-moderu 動態経営モデル dynamic management model
dōteki-buai 動的歩合 dynamic ratio
dōteki-hyōkahō 動的評価法 dynamic evaluation
dōteki-kanri-moderu 動的管理モデル dynamic managemnt model
dōteki-keikakuhō 動的計画法 dynamic programming
dōteki-ningen-kankei-kenkyū 動的人間関係研究

sociometric

dosū-bunpu 度数分布
frequency distribution

dōtai-hiritsu 動態比率
dynamic ratio

E

eigyōbu 営業部 sales department
eigyō-ken 営業権 goodwill
eigyō-meisaihyō 営業明細表 business portfolio
eigyō-menkyo 営業免許 franchise
eigyō-menkyo o ataeru 営業免許を与える franchise *v.*
eigyō-seisaku 営業政策 business policy
eikyō 影響 impact
eiri-hōjin 営利法人 business corporation
eisei-yōin 衛生要因 hygiene factors
eizō de mirareru tekisuto 映像でみられるテキスト teletext
eizō-hyōji-sōchi 映像表示装置 display unit (computer)

F

fakkusu ファックス fax
fakkusu o okuru ファックスを送る fax *v.*
fakkusu-kiki ファックス機器 fax machine
fīdo-bakku フィードバック feedback
fuka-kachi 付加価値 value added
fuka-kachi-zei 付加価値税 value added tax (VAT)
fukakutei-yōso 不確定要素 X factor
fuka-ritsu 負荷率 load factor
fukko-senryaku 復古戦略 reactive strategy
fukōsei na kyōsō 不公正な競争 unfair competition
fuku-kaichō 副会長 vice-chairman
fuku-sanbutsu 副産物 by-product
fuku-shachō 副社長 vice-president
fuku-shihainin 副支配人 assistant manager
fukugō-seisanbutsu 複合生産物 product mix
fukugyō 副業 moonlighting
fukusū-kyōkyūgen 複数供給源 dual sourcing
fukyō-ka no infure 不況下のインフレ stagflation
funshoku-teian 粉飾提案 window dressing
funsō-chōteinin 紛争調停人 trouble shooter
furikae-kakaku 振替価格 transfer pricing
furoppī フロッピー floppy
furoppī-disuku フロッピーディスク floppy disk
furyō-saiken 不良債権 bad debts
fusai ni yoru shikin-chōtatsu 負債による資金調達 debt financing
fusai no ryūdō 負債の流動 negative cash flow
fusai-kanri 負債管理 asset liability management
fusai-tai-shihon-ritsu 負債対資本率 debt-equity ratio
fusei-shikin 不正資金 slush fund
fushin 不振 slack, slump
fushin-bumon o kirisuteru 不振部門を切り捨てる slim down *v.*
fusoku-seisan-nōryoku 不足生産能力 undercapacity
futō-kaiko 不当解雇 unfair dismissal
futō-renbai 不当廉売 dumping
fuyōbutsu no jokyo 不要物の除去 descaling

G

gaibu ni hatchū-suru 外部に発注する contract out *v.*
gaibu-haichi 外部配置 outplacement
gaichū-suru 外注する externalize, put out-house *v.*
gaisū de 概数で in round figures
gaiyō-setsumei 概要説明 briefing
gakugai deno gakushū 学外での学習 distance learning
gakumen 額面 par
gakumen de 額面で at par
gakumen-ijō 額面以上 above par
gakumen-ika 額面以下 below par
gakushū-kyokusen 学習曲線 learning curve
gankin-kaishū 元金回収 payback
gappei 合併 amalgamation, merger
gēmu no namae ゲームの名前 name of the game
gēmu no riron ゲームの理論 game theory
gēto'uei ゲートウエイ gateway
genba 現場 shop floor
genba-iken-saiyō-senryaku 現場意見採用戦略 bottom-up strategy
genbutsu-kakaku 現物価格 spot price
genchi-buhin-shiyō-kisoku 現地部品使用規則 local content rules
genchi-chōsa 現地調査 field research
genchika 現地化 localization
gengo-komyunikēshon 言語コミュニケーション verbal communication
genka no haibun 原価の配分 allocation of costs
genka-bumon 原価部門 cost centre
genka-bunseki 原価分析 cost analysis
genka-chūshinten 原価中心点 cost centre
genka-hikisage 原価引き下げ cost reduction
genka-ishiki 原価意識 cost awareness, cost consciousness
genka-kaikei 原価会計 cost accounting
genka-kanri 原価管理 cost control
genka-keisan 原価計算 cost accounting, costing
genka-kijun 原価基準 cost standard
genka-kōsei 原価構成 cost structure
genka-sagaku 原価差額 cost variance
genka-sai 原価差異 cost variance
genka-shōkyaku-hikiatekin 原価償却引当金 depreciation allowance
genka-shōkyaku-suru 原価償却する depreciate *v.*
genka-uriage-rieki-bunseki 原価売上利益分析 cost-volume-profit analysis

genkahō 現価法 present value method
genkai-bunseki 限界分析 marginal analysis
genkai-genka-keisan 限界原価計算 marginal costing
genkai-hiyō 限界費用 marginal cost
genkai-hiyō-keisan 限界費用計算 marginal costing
genkai-kakaku-kettei 限界価格決定 marginal pricing
genkai-riekiritsu 限界利益率 profit volume ratio (P/V)
genkai-ryō 限界量 critical mass
genkin-barai (-shugi) 現金払(主義) pay as you go
genkin-busoku-jōtai 現金不足状態 cash poor
genkin-hippaku 現金逼迫 cash-strapped
genkin-hiritsu 現金比率 cash ratio
genkin-kanri 現金管理 cash management
genkin-ryūdō 現金流動 cash flow
genkin-shiharai 現金支払 disbursement
genkin-shūshi-waribiki 現金収支割引 discounted cash flow (DCF)
genkin-shūshi-yosan 現金収支予算 cash budget
genkin-shūshi-yosan-hensei 現金収支予算編成 cash budgeting
genkin-torihiki 現金取引 cash deal
genkō-buai 現行歩合 going rate
genkō-kinri 現行金利 going rate
genkyō-hōkokusho 現況報告書 status report
genmō-shisan 減耗資産 wasting assets
gensai-kikin 減債基金 sinking fund
gensen oyobi shito-shikin 源泉および使途資金 source and disposition of funds
gentei-kikan-hanbai 限定期間販売 sell by date
genzei 減税 tax relief
gidai ni ireru 議題に入れる to be on the agenda
giji-sagyō 疑似作業 dummy activity
gijutsu-iten 技術移転 technology transfer
gijutsu-ryoku 技術力 technological force
gijutsu-sekkeibu 技術設計部 engineering and design department
gijutsu-yosō 技術予想 technological forecasting
gijutsusha 技術者 engineer
ginkō-kinri 銀行金利 bank rate
ginō-bunseki 技能分析 skills analysis
go no ichikubun 語の一区分 byte
gokansei ga aru 互換性がある compatible
gomakasu ごまかす fiddle *v.*
gōben-gaisha 合弁会社 consortium, joint venture company
gōben-kigyō 合弁企業 joint venture

gōdō-daihyō (sei) 合同代表（制） joint representation
gōdō-rōshi-kōshō 合同労使交渉 joint negotiation
gōdō-suru 合同する amalgamate *v.*
gōi 合意 consensus
gōin na hanbai 強引な販売 hard selling
gōin na urikata 強引な売り方 hard sell
gōrika 合理化 rationalization
gurēpu-bain グレープ・バイン grapevine
gūhatsu 偶発 contingency
gūhatsu-riron 偶発理論 contingency theory
gūhatsu-sonshitsu-hikiatekin 偶発損失引当金 contingency reserve
gūhatsusei 偶発性 contingencies
gyaku-shotoku-zei 逆所得税 negative income tax
gyōmu 業務 job
gyōmu-bunseki 業務分析 operations breakdown
gyōmu-chōsa 業務調査 operations research (OR), work study
gyōmu-hōkoku 業務報告 policy statement
gyōmu-hyō 業務表 activity chart
gyōmu-hyōka 業務評価 performance evaluation
gyōmu-kaizen-katsudō 業務改善活動 organization and methods (O&M)
gyōmu-kanri 業務管理 operating management
gyōmu-kansa 業務監査 operations audit
gyōmu-kansoka 業務簡素化 work simplification
gyōmu-keikaku 業務計画 operational planning
gyōmu-mihon 業務見本 activity sampling
gyōmu-naiyō 業務内容 work content
gyōmu-sashizusho 業務指図書 mission statement
gyōmu-senryaku 業務戦略 business strategy
gyōmu-shori-bunseki 業務処理分析 transactional analysis (TA)
gyōmu-shōkai 業務招介 job profile
gyōmu-tanjunka 業務単純化 job simplification
gyōmu-teian 業務提案 business proposal
gyōmu-yosan (-sakusei) 業務予算（作成） performance budgeting
gyōseki-hyōka 業績評価 performance appraisal
gyōseki-kijun 業績基準 performance standards
gyōseki-satei 業績査定 performance evaluation
gyōseki-sokutei 業績測定 performance measurement

H

hādo-disuku ハード・ディスク hard disk
hādo-kopī ハード・コピー hard copy
hādouea ハードウエア hardware
haibun 配分 apportionment, distribution
haichi-suru 配置する deploy *v.*
haichi-tenkan 配置転換 job rotation
haiteku ハイテク high tech
haitō 配当 dividend
haitō-seisaku 配当政策 dividend policy
hakkō-zumi-kabushiki shihonkin 発行済み株式資本金 issued capital
han-jukurenkō 半熟練工 semi-skilled labour
hanbai-apīru 販売アピール sales appeal
hanbai-bēsu 販売ベース point of sale
hanbai-chiiki 販売地域 sales area
hanbai-chiten kara no denshi-sōkin 販売地点からの電子送金 EFTOPS (electric funds transfer at point of sale)
hanbai-hōshin 販売方針 distribution policy
hanbai-jiten 販売時点 point-of-sale
hanbai-kaiten-ritsu 販売回転率 sales turnover
hanbai-kakuchō-doryoku 販売拡張努力 sales expansion effort
hanbai-kakuchō-undō 販売拡張運動 sales drive
hanbai-kanōryō 販売可能量 sales potential
hanbai-kanri 販売管理 sales management
hanbai-kanrisha 販売管理者 distribution manager
hanbai-kasho-senden 販売箇所宣伝 point-of-sale advertising
hanbai-keikaku 販売計画 sales planning
hanbai-kuiki 販売区域 sales territory
hanbai-mitsumori 販売見積 sales forecast
hanbai-mokuhyō 販売目標 sales goal
hanbai-mōshikomi 販売申込 tender
hanbai-rieki 販売利益 return on sales
hanbai-seisaku 販売政策 sales policy
hanbai-sekininsha 販売責任者 marketing manager, sales manager
hanbai-senryaku 販売戦略 marketing strategy
hanbai-shūeki-ritsu 販売収益率 return on sales
hanbai-sokushin 販売促進 sales drive, impulse sales
hanbai-sokushin (-saku) 販売促進（策） sales promotion
hanbai-sokushin-katsudō 販売促進活動 merchandising
hanbai-sokushin-seisaku 販売促進政策 promotional

policy
hanbai-sokushin-sōgō shudan 販売促進総合手段 promotional mix
hanbai-sokushin-yōso no ketsugō 販売促進予想の結合 sales mix
hanbai-sokyū 販売訴求 sales appeal
hanbai-wariate (-ryō) 販売割当（量） sales quota
hanbai-yōso no ketsugō 販売予想の結合 marketing mix
hanbai-yosoku 販売予測 sales budget
hanbai-yosō 販売予想 sales expectations
hanbairyō 販売量 sales volume
hanbairyoku 販売力 sales force
handōtai 半導体 semi-conductor
hannō 反応 reactive
hantei-bunseki 判定分析 decision analysis
hassō-suru 発送する route *v.*
hatten-nōryoku no aru 発展能力のある viable
hatten-senzairyoku 発展潜在力 development potential
heigō-suru 併合する merge *v.*
heikin-genka 平均原価 average cost
heikin-hōshū 平均報酬 average yield
heikin-shūnyū 平均収入 average revenue
heikō-shakkan 平行借款 parallel loan
heikō-tsūka 平行通貨 parallel currency
heikō-yunyū 平行輸入 parallel import
heiten-hiyō 閉店費用 closing-down costs
heikin-rimawari 平均利回り average yield
hendō-genka-keisan 変動原価計算 variable costing
henkō-kanri 変更管理 change management
hensai-suru 返済する repay *v.*
hi-chokketsu 非直結 off line
hi-eiri 非営利 non-profit-making
hi-gengo-komyunikēshon 非言語コミュニケーション non-verbal communication
hi-jōjō-kabushiki 非上場株式 unlisted security
hi-jōjō-kigyō 非上場企業 unlisted company
hi-jōkin-jūgyōin 非常勤従業員 part-timer, part-time employee
hi-jōkin-jūgyōin no koyō 非常勤従業員の雇用 part-time employment
hi-jōkin-torishimariyaku 非常勤取締役 non-executive-director
hi-kakakuteki-yōin 非価格的要因 non-price factors
hi-kanzei-shōheki 非関税障壁 non-tariff barrier (NTB)
hi-kōiteki-shiyōsha 非好意的使用者 user unfriendly
hi-kōnin-katsudō 非公認活動 unofficial action
hi-kōshiki-soshiki 非公式組織 informal organization
hi-kōshiki-sutoraiki 非公式ス

トライキ unofficial strike
hi-renzoku 非連続 off-stream
hi-senkei-keikakuhō 非線型計画法 non-linear programming
hi-taikeiteki na 非体系的な unstructured
hi-taikyūzai 非耐久財 non-durable goods
himitsu no rōei 秘密の漏洩 security leak
himitsu-kyōgi-jikō 秘密協議事項 hidden agenda
hinagiku-gata-sharin 雛菊型車輪 daisy wheel
hinode-sangyō 日の出産業 sunrise industry
hinshitsu 品質 quality
hinshitsu-hoshō 品質保証 quality assurance
hinshitsu-hyōka 品質評価 quality assessment
hinshitsu-kanri 品質管理 quality control (QC), quality management
hinshitsu-kanri-shō-gurūpu 品質管理小グループ quality circle
hinshu-kakudai 品種拡大 brand stretching
hinshu-sakugen 品種削減 variety reduction
hirei-shite 比例して *pro rata*
hitokabu-atari no shūeki 一株当たりの収益 earnings per share (EPS)
hiyō no yūkōsei 費用の有効性 cost efficient
hiyō-appaku-infure 費用圧迫インフレ cost-push inflation
hiyō-binkansei 費用敏感性 cost sensitive
hiyō-bunseki 費用分析 cost analysis
hiyō-haibun 費用配分 allocation of costs
hiyō-kōka 費用効果 cost-effectiveness
hiyō-kōka-bunseki 費用効果分析 cost-benefit analysis (CBA)
hiyō-kōritsu 費用効率 cost-efficient
hiyō-yōin 費用要因 cost factor
hojo-shisetsu 補助施設 back-up facility
hojoteki sagyō 補助的作業 ancillary operations
hojoteki-gyōmu 補助的業務 subsidiarity
honsha 本社 head office
hontai 本体 mainframe
hōhō-kenkyū 方法研究 methods study
hōhō-kōgaku 方法工学 methods engineering
hōhōronteki-gensoku-shugi 方法論的原則主義 organogram
hōjin-zei 法人税 corporate tax
hōkai 崩壊 disintegration
hōkatsu-kōshō 包括交渉 package deal
hosa-sei 補佐制 staff assistant
hōshin no jisshi 方針の実施 policy execution
hōshin no kōshikika 方針の公式化 policy formulation
hoshōkin-ritsu 保証金率 cover ratio
hoshu 保守 maintenance
hōshū 報酬 remuneration, yield
hōsō 包装 packaging

hotto-manē ホット・マネー hot money
howaito-karā ホワイトカラー white collar workers
hyōji-sōchi 表示装置 visual display unit (VDU)
hyōjun-genka 標準原価 standard costs
hyōjun-genka-keisan 標準原価計算 standard costing
hyōjun-hensa 標準偏差 standard deviation
hyōjun-hiyō 標準費用 standard costs
hyōjun-jikan 標準時間 standard time
hyōjun-sagyō 標準作業 standard performance
hyōjun-sagyōryō 標準作業量 workload
hyōjunka 標準化 standardization
hyōjunka-suru 標準化する standardize *v.*
hyōka-suru 評価する appreciate, evaluate *v.*
hyōkagaku-teian 評価額提案 value proposal

I

ian-kyūka 慰安休暇 comfort break
ichi-hyōji-kikō 位置表示機構 cursor
ichiji-kaiko 一時解雇 lay-off
ichiji-kaiko-suru 一時解雇する lay off *v.*
ichiji-kin 一時金 lump sum
ichiji-sanpin 一次産品 primary commodity
ichijirushii zōka 著しい増加 upswing
ichinichi-kōtai-sei 一日交代制 day shift
ichiranhyō 一覧表 vision statement
ichiritsu-shōkyū 一律昇給 across the board increase
ichiryū-shōken 一流証券 gilt-edged security
idōshiki-denwa 移動式電話 mobile phone
igi-bukai 意義深い significant
iji-nōryoku 維持能力 sustainability
iken-jōshin-senryaku 意見上申戦略 bottom-up strategy
ikinokori-senryaku 生き残り戦略 survival strategy
ikkatsu-keiyaku 一括契約 bulk contract
ikkatsu-seisan 一括生産 batch production
ikkatsu-shori 一括処理 batch processing
ikkatsu-suru 一括する package *v.* (to…a policy)
imi no aru 意味のある meaningful
infure-atsuryoku インフレ圧力 inflationary pressure
inputto インプット input
insaidā-torihiki インサイダー取引 insider dealing, insider trading
insatsu-shutsuryoku 印刷出力 printout
insatsu-suru 印刷する print out *v.*
intāfēsu インターフェース interface
intai 引退 retirement
intai-suru 引退する retire v.
ishi-kettei no keitōzu 意志決定の系統図 decision tree
ishi-kettei-purosesu 意志決定プロセス decision process
ishi-kettei-riron 意志決定理論 decision theory
ishi-kettei-moderu 意志決定モデル decision model

J

janku-bondo ジャンクボンド junk bond
jasuto-in-taimu ジャスト・イン・タイム just in time (JIT)
jibunkatsu (shori) 時分割（処理） time sharing
jidō-dētā-shori 自動データー処理 automatic data processing (ADP)
jidōka-suru 自動化する automate *v.*
jidōsha-denwa 自動車電話 car phone
jigyō-bumon 事業部門 operating division, operations
jigyō-bumon-kanri 事業部門管理 operations management
jigyō-gaisha 事業会社 business corporation
jigyō-keikaku 事業計画 operational planning
jigyōtai 事業体 business unit
jika-hōshiki 時価方式 present value method
jikan no jōkyō 時間の状況 time phase
jikan no okure 時間の遅れ time-lag
jikan no zure 時間のずれ time-lag
jikan oyobi dōsa-kenkyū 時間および動作研究 time and motion study
jikan oyobi hōhō-kenkyū 時間および方法研究 time and methods study
jikan-kanri 時間管理 time management
jikan-kenkyū 時間研究 time study
jikan-kōsei 時間構成 time frame
jikan-shinshuku-shukkinsei 時間伸縮出勤制 flexitime
jikeiretsu 時系列 time series
jiki-disuku 磁気ディスク magnetic disk
jikken-shijō 実験市場 test marketing
jiko-happun 自己発憤 self-motivation
jiko-hyōka 自己評価 self-appraisal
jiko-jitsugenka 自己実現化 self-actualization
jiko-kaishū 自己回収 self-liquidating
jiko-kin'yū 自己金融 self-financing
jiko-shihon 自己資本 net worth
jikoku 自国 home country
jimu-jidōka 事務自動化 office automation
jimu-jikan-sokutei 事務時間測定 clerical work measurement (CWM)
jimu-kaizen-keikaku 事務改善計画 office planning
jimu-kanri 事務管理 office management
jimu-keikaku 事務計画 office planning
jimu-shokuin 事務職員 clerical workers
jimusho 事務所 office
jin'in-busoku 人員不足 undermanning
jin'in-busoku no 人員不足の undermanned

jin'in-haichi 人員配置 manning
jin'in-hyō 人員表 manpower audit
jin'in-kajō 人員過剰 overmanning
jin'in-keikaku 人員計画 manpower planning
jin'in-sakugen 人員削減 demanning
jinji-hōshin 人事方針 personnel policy
jinji-idō 人事異動 staff transfers
jinji-kanri 人事管理 personnel management
jinji-kōsa 人事考査 personnel rating
jinji-seisaku 人事政策 personnel policy
jinji-tantōsha 人事担当者 personnel manager
jinjibu 人事部 personnel department
jinkō-chinō 人工知能 artificial intelligence
jinteki-seichō 人的成長 personal growth
jinteki-shigen 人的資源 human resources, manpower resources
jinteki-shigen-kaihatsu 人的資源開発 human resource development
jinteki-shigen-kanri 人的資源管理 human resource
jōkin-koyō 常勤雇用 full-time employment
jōkinsha 常勤者 full-time employee
jūgyōin-busoku 従業員不足 understaffing
jūgyōin-kaunseringu 従業員カウンセリング employee counselling
jūgyōin-keiei-sanka 従業員経営参加 worker participation
jūgyōin-keiyaku 従業員契約 staff commitment
jūgyōin-kyōkyū 従業員供給 staff resourcing
jūgyōin-saiyō-keikaku 従業員採用計画 staff planning
jūgyōin-sakugen 従業員削減 personnel reductions, downsizing
jūgyōin-sanka-keiei 従業員参加経営 participative management
jūgyōin-satei 従業員査定 staff inspection
jūgyōin-shikakusho 従業員資格書 personnel specification
jūyakukai 重役会 board of directors
juyō-infure 需要インフレ demand-pull inflation
juyō-satei 需要査定 demand assessment
juyō-yosoku 需要予測 demand forecasting

K

kabuka-shūekiritsu 株価収益率 price earnings ratio (P/E)
kabunushi-ken 株主権 equity
kabunushi-wariate-hakkō 株主割り当て発行 rights issue
kabunushi-ken no kishaku 株主権の希釈 dilution of equity
kabushiki o kōbo-suru 株式を公募する go public *v.*
kabushiki-kaiire-sentakuken 株式買い入れ選択権 stock option
kabushiki-kōkai-kaitsuke 株式公開買い付け take-over bid (TOB)
kabushiki-kōkai-kigyō 株式公開企業 publicly listed company
kabushiki-nakagaigyō 株式仲買業 stockbroking
kabushiki-nakagainin 株式仲買人 stockbroker
kabushiki-shihon 株式資本 share capital
kabushiki-shijō 株式市場 equity market
kabushiki-sōba no jissei 株式相場の実勢 price performance
kabushiki-yūsen-kaitori-sentakuken (-seido) 株式優先買取選択権（制度） stock option plan
kachi 価値 value
kachi-bunseki 価値分析 value analysis (VA)
kachi-gainen 価値概念 value concept
kachi-kōgaku 価値工学 value engineering
kachi-taikei 価値体系 value chain
kadai 課題 job challenge
kadai-shihonka (sareta) 過大資本化（された） overcapitalized
kaeru-tobi-sōba 蛙飛び相場 leapfrogging
kagakuteki-kanri (hō) 科学的管理（法） scientific management
kagakuteki-puroguramingu 科学的プログラミング scientific programming
kahenhi 可変費 variable costs
kahensei 可変制 variance
kai no kazu o kirisuteru 下位の数を切り捨てる round off *v.*
kaichō 会長 chairman
kaichō-dairi 会長代理 deputy chairman
kaidoku-suru 解読する unscramble *v.*
kaigai-tōshi 海外投資 off-shore investment
kaigishitsu 会議室 board-room
kaigyō 開業 start-up
kaigyō-hiyō 開業費用 start-up costs
kaihatsu-gyōsha 開発業者 developer
kaihatsu-keikaku 開発計画 development programme
kaihatsu-yosō no ketsugō 開発予想の結合 promotional mix
kaihō-keikaku 開放計画 open plan
kaihōshiki no 開放式の open

ended

kaihōshiki-tsūshinmō-setsubi 開放式通信網設備 open network provision

kaiire 買入 buyout

kaikaku 改革 innovatory

kaikaku-suru 改革する innovate *v.*

kaikakuteki 改革的 innovative

kaikata-shijō 買い方市場 bull market

kaikei-hiritsu 会計比率 accounting ratio

kaikei-kansa 会計監査 audit

kaikei-kansakan 会計監査官 comptroller

kaikei-kikan 会計期間 accounting period

kaikei-moderu 会計モデル accounting model

kaikei-nendo 会計年度 financial year, fiscal year

kaikei-sekinin 会計責任 accountables

kaikei-sekininsha 会計責任者 chief accountant

kaiketsu-suru 解決する solve *v.*

kaiki-bunseki 回帰分析 regression analysis

kaiko 解雇 pay-off, dismissal, firing

kaiko-suru 解雇する fire *v.*

kaisan 解散 dissolution, liquidation

kaisha e teire-suru 会社へ手入れする raid a company *v.*

kaisha no hōshin 会社の方針 company policy

kaisha no shinboru-māku 会社のシンボル・マーク company logo

kaishi 開始 launching

kaishime 買い占め corner

kaishimeru 買い占める corner *v.*

kaishū-kikan 回収期間 pay-back period

kaitaku-suru 開拓する pioneer *v.*

kaite-shijō 買い手市場 buyer's market, bull market

kaiten-shin'yō-kanjō 回転信用勘定 revolving credit

kaitoru 買い取る buy out *v.*

kajō-jin'in-haichi 過剰人員配置 overmanned

kajō-jūgyōin 過剰従業員 overstaffing

kajō-kakudai 過剰拡大 overextended

kajō-seisan-nōryoku 過剰生産能力 overcapacity

kajō-setsubi 過剰設備 excess capacity

kajō-shokuin-koyō 過剰職員雇用 overstaffing

kajū-bairitsu 荷重倍率 load factor

kajū-heikin 加重平均 weighted average

kakaku o kimeru 価格を決める price *v.*

kakaku o sageru 価格を下げる underpriced *v.*

kakaku o sayū-suru jōhō 価格を左右する情報 price sensitive information

kakaku-binkansei 価格敏感性 cost sensitive

kakaku-bunri 価格分離 unbundling

kakaku-chōsei 価格調整 price adjustment

kakaku-jōshō 価格上昇 price escalation
kakaku-kakusa 価格格差 price differential
kakaku-kettei 価格決定 price determination, pricing
kakaku-kettei-hōshin 価格決定方針 pricing policy
kakaku-kettei-senryaku 価格決定戦略 pricing strategy
kakaku-kettei-yōin 価格決定要因 price factor
kakaku-kirisage 価格切り下げ price cutting
kakaku-kōsei 価格構成 price structure
kakaku-kyōtei 価格協定 price fixing
kakaku-sabetsu 価格差別 price discrimination
kakaku-sendōsha 価格先導者 price leader
kakaku-shisū 価格指数 price index
kakaku-shūeki-ritsu 価格収益率 price earnings ratio (P/E)
kakaku-teiji 価格提示 value proposal
kakaku-tsuizuisha 価格追随者 price follower
kake-tsunagi-sōsa かけつなぎ操作 hedging operation
kakoikomu 囲み込む ring fence *v.*
kakō 下降 downturn
kakō-gata-senryaku 下降型戦略 top-down strategy
kakō-kyokumen 下降局面 downswing
kakō-sōba 下降相場 down market
kakō-suru 加工する process *v.*
kakuchō-gyōmu 拡張業務 extension services
kakudai-senryaku 拡大戦略 expansion strategy
kakudai-suru 拡大する expand *v.*
kakuritsu-riron 確率理論 probability theory
kakusa-kenkyū 格差研究 gap study
kakusareta-gidai 隠された議題 hidden agenda
kakushi-shisan 隠し資産 hidden assets
kakutei-kenri 確定権利 vested interest
kakutoku 獲得 acquisitions
kakutoku-suru 獲得する acquire *v.*
kanbu oyobi rain-yōin 幹部およびライン要員 staff and line
kanbu-jinzai-yōsei-senryaku 幹部人材養成戦略 executive manpower strategy
kanbu-shokuin no kaiko 幹部職員の解雇 golden handshake
kanbu-shokuin no kaiko-teate 幹部職員の解雇手当 golden parachute
kanbu-shokuin-senryaku 幹部職員戦略 executive staff strategy
kando-bunseki 感度分析 sensitivity analysis
kanekashi 金貸し lombard
kanjusei-kunren 感受性訓練 sensitivity training
kankatsuken 管轄権 jurisdiction
kankin-suru 換金する liquidate *v.*
kankō 慣行 custom and practice

kankyō 環境 environment
kankyō-bunseki 環境分析 environmental analysis
kankyō-chōsa 環境調査 environmental scan
kankyō-mondai 環境問題 green issues
kankyō-yosoku 環境予測 environmental forecasting
kanmei ni setsumei-suru 簡明に説明する brief *v.*
kannō-bunseki 感応分析 sensitivity analysis
kannō-kunren 感応訓練 sensitivity training
kanren-saseru 関連させる correlate *v.*
kanri 管理 administration, control
kanri-gyōmu 管理業務 management services
kanri-han'i 管理範囲 span of control
kanri-hōshiki 管理方式 managerial style
kanri-iinkai 管理委員会 board control
kanri-kagaku 管理科学 management science
kanri-kaikei 管理会計 management accounting
kanri-kanō-hiyō 管理可能費用 managed costs
kanri-keiei-hiritsu 管理経営比率 administration-production ratio
kanri-kikō 管理機構 managerial structure
kanri-kinō 管理機能 managerial function
kanri-kōka 管理効果 managerial effectiveness
kanri-kōzō 管理構造 managerial structure
kanri-nōryoku 管理能力 executive competence
kanri-sareta 管理された managed
kanri-shokeihi 管理諸経費 administrative overheads
kanri-suru 管理する manage *v.*
kanri-zuhyō 管理図表 management chart
kanrisha 管理者 supervisor
kanrisha no kengen 管理者の権限 line authority
kanrishoku 管理職 controller, executive
kanrishoku no shōshin 管理職の昇進 executive advancement
kanrishoku (-kakutoku)-senryaku 管理職（獲得）戦略 executive manpower strategy
kanrishoku-saiyō 管理職採用 executive search
kanrishoku-saiyō-jigyō 管理職採用事業 executive search
kanriteki-tōsei 管理的統制 managerial control
kansa-suru 監査する audit *v.*
kansatsu no kikai 観察の機会 window of opportunity
kansayaku 監査役 auditor
kansayō-puroguramu-tekiyō-gyōmu 監査用プログラム適用業務 software application
kansetsu-hiyō 間接費用 indirect cost
kansetsu-keihi 間接経費 indirect expenses
kansetsu-rōdō 間接労働 indirect labour
kansetsu-rōdō-hi 間接労働費

indirect labour expenses
kansetsuhi 間接費 indirect expenses
kansetsuhi-kachi-bunseki 間接費価値分析 overhead value analysis (OVA)
kansetsuhi-kaishū 間接費回収 overhead recovery
kanshi-kanri 監視管理 supervisory management
kanshi-suru 監視する monitor *v.*
kanshō-zaiko 緩衝在庫 buffer stock
kantoku 監督 foreman
kantoku-suru 監督する supervise *v.*
kanzan (-gaku) 換算（額） conversion (foreign exchange)
kanzei-shōheki 関税障壁 tariff barrier
kanzen ni 完全に down the line
karuteru カルテル cartel
kasan-teate 加算手当 weighting
kashi-daore-sonshitsu 貸し倒れ損失 bad-debt losses
kashitsuke-shihon 貸付資本 loan capital
kashobun-shotoku 可処分所得 disposable income
kashō-shihon 過小資本 undercapitalized
kashō-sōgyō 過小操業 underperform
kasseika-suru 活性化する activate *v.*
katokiteki 過渡期的 transitional
katsudō-chūshutsu (-chōsa) 活動抽出（調査） activity sampling
katsudō-han'i 活動範囲 niche
kattingu-ejji カッティング・エッジ cutting edge
kawakami (-sangyō) 川上（産業） upstream
kawase-satei 為替査定 arbitrage
kawase-shijō 為替市場 Exchange Rate Mechanism (ERM)
kawashimo (-sangyō) 川下（産業） downstream
kazei-kōjo 課税控除 tax deductible
kazei-suru 課税する tax *v.*
kazoku-keitōzu 家族系統図 family tree
keiei (jin) 経営（陣） management
keiei no keizoku 経営の継続 management succession
keiei-chīmu 経営チーム management team
keiei-gakusha 経営学者 business economist
keiei-gijutsu 経営技術 management techniques
keiei-hikaku 経営比較 inter-firm comparison
keiei-hiritsu 経営比率 management ratio
keiei-hōhōron 経営方法論 systems and procedures
keiei-hōshin 経営方針 business policy
keiei-jōhō 経営情報 management information
keiei-jōhō-chōsa-seido 経営情報調査制度 management information system (MIS)
keiei-kagaku 経営科学 management science

keiei-kankō 経営慣行 management practices
keiei-kanōsei 経営可能性 management potential
keiei-kanri-gihō 経営管理技法 management techniques
keiei-kanri-hōhō 経営管理方法 administrative control procedure
keiei-kanri-riron 経営管理理論 administrative theory, management theory
keiei-kansa 経営監査 management audit
keiei-keiyaku 経営契約 management contract
keiei-konsarutanto 経営コンサルタント management consultant
keiei-konsarutanto-gyō 経営コンサルタント業 management consultancy
keiei-riron 経営理論 administrative theory, management theory
keiei-seisan-ritsu 経営生産率 administration-production ratio
keiei-senryaku 経営戦略 business strategy, business stream
keiei-shidō 経営指導 management services
keiei-soshiki 経営組織 management system, business system
keieisha 経営者 manager
keieisha no jisha-kaitori 経営者の自社買取 management buyout
keieisha no senzai-nōryoku 経営者の潜在能力 management potential
keieisha-kaihatsu 経営者開発 executive development
keiei-keishō 経営継承 management succession
keisūka 計数化 digitizing (computer)
keihi 経費 overheads
keihi-kaishū 経費回収 overheads recovery
keihi-sakugen 経費削減 cost reduction
keijōhi 経常費 current expenditure
keikaku o hōki-suru 計画を放棄する chunk a project *v.*
keikaku (-sakutei) 計画（策定） planning
keikaku-betsu-yosansei 計画別予算性 programme budgeting
keikaku-kanri 計画管理 project management
keikakuteki-chinpuka 計画的陳腐化 planned obsolescence
keikakuteki-hoshu 計画的保守 planned maintenance
keikakuteki-jininsakugen 計画的人員削減 demanning
keikakuteki-kei'ei-kanri 計画的経営管理 programmed management
keikakuteki-kekkin 計画的欠勤 absenteeism
keiki no junkan 景気の循環 business cycle
keiki-dōkō 景気動向 business stream
keiki-junkan 景気循環 business cycle
keiki-yosoku 景気予測 business forecasting
keireki-keikaku 経歴計画 career planning

keiretsu-gaisha 系列会社 associate(d) company
keiri 経理 accounting
keiro 経路 route
keiryō-bunseki 計量分析 quantitative analysis
keiryō-keizaigakuteki 計量経済学的 econometric
keisūka-suru 計数化する digitize *v.*
keitai-bunseki 形態分析 morphological analysis
keiyaku ni tassuru 契約に達する reach a deal *v.*
keiyakuryō 契約量 production run
keizai-batchi-sūryō 経済バッチ数量 economic batch quantity
keizai-chōsa 経済調査 economic research
keizai-dōkō 経済動向 economic trend
keizai-jōhō 経済情報 economic intelligence
keizai-kikendo 経済危険度 economic exposure
keizai-kishō 経済気象 economic climate
keizai-seichō-yokusei-yōin 経済成功抑制要因 disincentive
keizai-shisetsudan 経済使節団 economic mission
keizoku-kiroku-tanaoroshi (-seido) 継続記録棚卸し（制度） perpetual inventory
keizokuteki-zaikohin-shirabe 継続的在庫品調べ continuous stocktaking
keizu 系図 family tree
keiribu 経理部 accounting department
keitai-denwa 携帯電話 cellphone
keiyaku-gyōmu 契約業務 work by contract
keiyaku-koyō 契約雇用 contract hire
keizai-seichō-sogai (-yōin) 経済成長阻害（要因） disincentive
kekka ni taishite oubeki gimu 結果に対して負うべき義務 accountability
kenbō-jussū 権謀術数 wheeling and dealing
kengen no shukushō 権限の縮小 contraction of authority
kengen-han'i 権限範囲 arm's length
kenkyū-kaihatsu 研究開発 research and development (R & D)
kenkyū-kaihatsubu 研究開発部 research department
ken'nin-jūyaku 兼任重役 interlocking directorate
ken'nin-torishimariyaku 兼任取締役 interlocking directorate
kenryoku no seigen 権力の制限 contraction of authority
kenryoku-kōzō 権力構造 authority structure
kenshō-shiryō 検証資料 viewdata
kēsu-sutadī ケーススタディ case study
ketsuzō 結像 imaging
kiban-soshiki 基盤組織 matrix organizations
kibo no fukeizaisei 規模の不経済性 diseconomy of scale
kibo no keizaisei 規模の経済性 economy of scale
kigō 記号 logo

kigyō 企業 enterprise
kigyō no hōshiki 企業の方式 house style
kigyō no kaisan 企業の解散 demerger
kigyō no kyūshū-gappei 企業の吸収合併 mergers and acquisitions (M&A)
kigyō no seichō 企業の成長 corporate growth
kigyō no tōgōteki na mokuteki 企業の統合的な目的 overall company objectives
kigyō-bunka 企業文化 corporate culture
kigyō-dōtaigaku 企業動態学 industrial dynamics
kigyō-gaiyō 企業概要 company profile
kigyō-gōdō 企業合同 syndicate
kigyō-heisa 企業閉鎖 winding up
kigyō-himitsu 企業秘密 company secret
kigyō-hōshin 企業方針 company policy
kigyō-imēji 企業イメージ corporate image
kigyō-keiei 企業経営 business management, venture management
kigyō-keikaku 企業計画 company planning, corporate planning
kigyō-kōkoku 企業広告 corporate advertising
kigyō-kōzō 企業構造 corporate structure
kigyō-māku 企業マーク company logo
kigyō-moderu 企業モデル corporate model
kigyō-mokuhyō 企業目標 company goal
kigyō-mokuteki 企業目的 company goal, company objective
kigyō-saiken 企業再建 company reconstruction
kigyō-seichō 企業成長 corporate growth
kigyō-seishin ni tomu 企業精神に富む enterprising
kigyō-senryaku 企業戦略 corporate strategy
kigyō-shūeki 企業収益 company profit
kigyō-tetsugaku 企業哲学 company philosophy
kigyō-zentai no seichō 企業全体の成長 organic growth
kigyōka-seishin 企業家精神 entrepreneurial spirit
kigyōnai-kunren 企業内訓練 training within industry (TWI)
kihon-ryōkin 基本料金 base rate
kijun 基準 standard
kijun-nenji 基準年次 base year
kijun-rikai no gimu 基準理解の義務 need-to-know basis
kijun-shakudo 基準尺度 yardstick
kikai no shudan 機会の手段 window of opportunity
kikai-gengo 機械言語 machine language
kikai-hiyō 機会費用 opportunity cost
kikai-kōdo 機械コード machine code
kikaku o umu 企画を生む generate ideas *v.*
kikaku-bunseki 企画分析

project analysis
kikaku-keikaku-yosan-hōshiki 企画計画予算方式 planning, programming, budgeting system (PPBS)
kikaku-sakutei 企画策定 project planning
kikakubu 企画部 planning department
kiken na kagaku-kagōbutsu 危険な化学化合物 hazchem (hazardous chemicals)
kiken o kyokushōka-suru 危険を極小化する minimize risks *v.*
kiken-bunseki 危険分析 risk analysis
kiken-futan-shihon 危険負担資本 venture capital
kiken-futan-shihonka 危険負担資本家 venture capitalist
kiken-gaisetsu 危険概説 risk profile
kiken-hyōka 危険評価 risk assessment
kiken-kanri 危険管理 risk management
kiken-purofīru 危険プロフィール risk profile
kiken-satei 危険査定 risk assessment
kiken-shihon 危険資本 risk capital
kikendo 危険度 exposure
kiki-kanri 危機管理 crisis management
kikō o saisei-suru 機構を再生する reinvent the wheel *v.*
kimitsu no rōei 機密の漏洩 security leak
kimitsusei 機密性 confidentiality
kin'yū-hikishime 金融引き締め credit squeeze
kin'yū-sakimono-torihiki 金融先物取引 financial futures
kin'yū-shijō 金融市場 financial market
kin'yū-sōsa 金融操作 financial management
kin'yūteki-shigeki 金融的刺激 financial incentive
kinchō o yawarageru kyūka 緊張を和らげる休暇 stretch break
kinchō-chūdan 緊張中断 stretch break
kinkō ni naru 均衡になる break even *v.*
kinkō no yoi shisan-naiyō 均衡のよい資産内容 balanced portfolio
kinkō-shisan (hyō) 均衡資産（表） balanced portfolio
kinmu-jikan 勤務時間 working hours
kinmu-jikan-kirokuhyō 勤務時間記録表 time sheet
kinō 機能 function
kinō-bunseki 機能分析 functional analysis, functional approach
kinō-furyō 機能不良 malfunction
kinō-haichi 機能配置 functional layout
kinō-kankei 機能関係 functional relations
kinō-kī 機能キー function key
kinō-kosuto (-keisan) 機能コスト（計算） functional costing
kinō-shōgai 機能障害

dysfunction
kinō-tenken 機能点検 functional approval
kinōhō 帰納法 induction
kinōteki 機能的 functional
kinōteki-haichi 機能的配置 functional layout
kinōteki-kakunin 機能的確認 functional approval
kinōteki-sekinin 機能的責任 functional responsibility
kinōteki-taiyō-nensū 機能的耐用年数 economic life
kioku 記憶 memory, store
kioku (-sōchi) 記憶（装置） memory
kioku-chippu 記憶チップ computer memory chip
kiremono 切れ者 whiz-kid
kirisage 切り下げ undercut
kisei 規制 regulation
kisei o kanwa-suru 規制を緩和する deregulate *v.*
kisei-kanwa 規制緩和 deregulation
kisei-suru 規制する regulate *v.*
kitoku-ken'eki 既得権益 vested interest
kō-chakuriku 硬着陸 hard landing
kō-kaiten-shōhi-busshi 高回転消費物資 fast moving consumer goods
kōbai-kōdō 購買行動 buying behaviour
kōbai-kyohi 購買拒否 consumer resistance
kōbai-tantōsha 購買担当者 chief buyer
kōbairyoku 購買力 purchasing power
kobetsu-bunseki-kunren 個別分析訓練 part-analysis training
kobetsu-genka-keisan 個別原価計算 product costing
kobetsu-keikaku 個別計画 project planning
kobetsu-seisan 個別生産 one-off
kodai-senden 誇大宣伝 hype
kōdo-gijutsu-suijun 高度技術水準 state of the art
kōdō-hōshin 行動方針 action plan
kōdō-kagaku 行動科学 behavioural science
kōdō-keikaku 行動計画 action plan
kōdō-nōryoku 行動能力 competency
kōei-kigyō 公営企業 public enterprise
kōen 後援 sponsorship
kogaisha 子会社 affiliate company, subsidiary company
kōgaku-gijutsu 工学技術 engineering
kōgo-tokkyo-shiyōken 交互特許使用権 cross licensing
kōgubako 工具箱 toolbox
koguchi-genkin 小口現金 petty cash
kōgyō-saiken 工業債券 industrial security
kōgyō-seihin 工業製品 industrial goods
kōgyōryoku no hakai 工業力の破壊 deindustrialization
kōhō 公報 public relations (PR)
kōhō-gyōmu no 後方業務の logistical
kōhō-gyōmu-katsudō 公報業

務活動 extension services
kōhō-katsudō 公報活動 public relations (PR)
kōhō-keijiban 公報掲示板 bulletin board
kōhō-shien-kōtei 後方支援工程 logistic process
kōhō-shien-tetsuzuki 後方支援手続き logistic process
kōhō-shiengaku 後方支援学 logistics
kōhosha-meibo 候補者名簿 shortlist
kōiki-nettowāku 広域ネットワーク wide area network (WAN)
kōiteki-shiyōsha 好意的使用者 user friendly
kōjō-betsu-kōshō 工場別交渉 plant bargaining
kojin-senyō ni suru 個人専用にする personalize *v.*
kojinteki-seichō 個人的成長 personal growth
kōjō-chintairyō 工場賃貸料 plant hire
kōjō-haichi-kenkyū 工場配置研究 plant layout study
kōjō-heisa 工場閉鎖 lockout
kōjō-iinkai 工場委員会 works committee
kōjō-jichō 工場次長 line assistant
kōjō-kanbu 工場幹部 shop steward
kōjō-kanrisha 工場管理者 works manager
kōjō-kansetsuhi 工場間接費 factory overhead
kōjō-keihi 工場経費 factory overheads
kōjō-nai-kunren 工場内訓練 in-plant training
kōjō-reberu no kōshō 工場レベルの交渉 plant bargaining
kōjō-shisetsu-haichi-kenkyū 工場施設配置研究 plant layout study
kōjō-shozaichi 工場所在地 plant location
kōjōchō 工場長 plant manager
kōkai-keikaku 公開計画 open plan
kōkai-shijō-sōsa 公開市場操作 open market operation
kōkai-tsūshinmōshisetsu 公開通信網施設 open network provision
kōkaiten-shōhi-busshi 高回転消費物資 fast-moving consumer goods (FMCG)
kōkan 交換 trade-off
kōkan-kanō-ōshū-tsūka 交換可能欧州通貨 hard ecu
kōkateki na kanri 効果的な管理 effective management
kōkeisha-keikaku 後継者計画 succession planning
kōkendo-bunseki 貢献度分析 contribution analysis
koko ni kakaku o tsukeru 個々に価格を付ける unbundle *v.*
kōkoku no shudai 広告の主題 advertising theme
kōkoku-baitai 広告媒体 advertising media
kōkoku-chōsa 広告調査 advertising research
kōkoku-dairiten 広告代理店 advertising agent
kōkoku-messēji 広告メッセージ advertising message
kōkoku-sekininsha 広告責任

者 advertising manager
kōkoku-yosan 広告予算 advertising budget
kōkokuhi 広告費 advertising appropriation
kokumin-sōseisan 国民総生産 gross national product (GNP)
kokusai ni yoru shikin-chōtatsu 国債による資金調達 debt financing
kokusai-reberu 国際レベル world class
kokusai-torihiki 国際取り引き global marketing
kokusaika-suru 国際化する internationalize *v.*
kokyaku ni taisuru hairyo 顧客に対する配慮 customer care
kokyaku-chūshin 顧客中心 customer-oriented
kokyaku-gaiyō 顧客概要 customer profile
kokyaku-hōshi 顧客奉仕 customer service
kokyaku-jōhō-teikyō 顧客情報提供 customer orientation
kokyaku-rijun 顧客利潤 customer profit
kokyaku-shidō 顧客指導 customer orientation
kokyaku-shikō 顧客志向 consumer intention
kōkyō-bumon-fusai-hensai 公共部門負債返済 public sector debt repayment (PSDR)
kōkyō-bumon-shakunyūkin-jōken 公共部門借入金条件 public sector borrowing (PSBR)
kōkyō-jigyō 公共事業 public utility
komon-gyōmu 顧問業務 advisory services
komon no 顧問の consultative
komyunikēshon-channeru コミュニケーションチャンネル channels of communication
kongō-tōshi 混合投資 investment mix
konguromaritto コングロマリット conglomerate
konpyūta コンピュータ computer
konpyūta ni motozuku kunren コンピュータに基づく訓練 computer-based training (CBT)
konpyūta ni yoru dezain コンピュータによるデザイン computer-aided design (CAD)
konpyūta ni yoru gakushū コンピュータによる学習 computer-aided learning (CAL)
konpyūta ni yoru kyōiku コンピュータによる教育 computer-assisted teaching (CAT)
konpyūta ni yoru seizō コンピュータによる製造 computer-aided manufacturing (CAM)
konpyūta ni yoru tōgō-seisan コンピュータによる統合生産 computer integrated manufacturing (CIM)
konpyūta no ayamari コンピュータの誤り bug
konpyūta-banku コンピュータバンク computer bank
konpyūta-bēsu no kunren-hōshiki コンピュータベースの訓練方式 computer based training (CBT)
konpyūta-gengo コンピュー

タ言語 computer language
konpyūta-jōhōriron コンピュータ情報理論 computer literate
konpyūta-jukurensha コンピュータ熟練者 computer expert
konpyūta-keisan コンピュータ計算 computer services
konpyūta-keisan-sentā コンピュータ計算センター computer services bureau
konpyūta-kioku (-sōchi) コンピュータ記憶（装置） computer memory
konpyūta-kioku-sōchi コンピュータ記憶装置 computer storage
konpyūta-konsarutanto コンピュータコンサルタント computer consultant
konpyūta-mattanki コンピュータ末端器 computer terminal
konpyūta-memori コンピュータ・メモリ computer memory
konpyūta-purogurumā コンピュータプログラマー computer programmer
konpyūta-puroguramingu コンピュータプログラミング computer programming
konpyūta-puroguramu コンピュータプログラム computer program
konpyūta-riyō-gakushū コンピュータ利用学習 computer-aided learning (CAL)
konpyūta-riyō-jōhō-shisutemu コンピュータ利用情報システム computerized information system (COINS)
konpyūta-riyō-kyōiku コンピュータ利用教育 computer-assisted teaching (CAT)
konpyūta-riyō-seizō コンピュータ利用製造 computer-aided manufacturing (CAM)
konpyūta-riyō-sekkei コンピュータ利用設計 computer-aided design (CAD)
konpyūta-sābisu コンピュータサービス computer services
konpyūta-senmonka コンピュータ専門家 computer expert system
konpyūta-sentā コンピュータセンター computer centre
konpyūta-shimyurēshon コンピュータシミュレーション computer simulation
konpyūta-tōgō-seisan コンピュータ統合生産 computer-integrated manufacturing (CIM)
konpyūta-uirusu コンピュータウイルス computer virus
konpyūta-yaburi コンピュータ破り hacker
konpyūtaka-suru コンピュータ化する computerize
konsarutanto コンサルタント consultant
konsarutanto-gyō コンサルタント業 consultancy
kontena コンテナ container
konsōshiamu コンソーシアム consortium
kontenaka コンテナ化 containerization
kōnyū 購入 purchasing
kōnyū-kanrisha 購入管理者 purchasing manager
kōnyū-sekininsha 購入責任

者 chief buyer
kōritsu-kansa 効率監査 efficiency audit
kōritsuka-suru 効率化する streamline *v.*
kōryū-bunseki 交流分析 transactional analysis (TA)
kōsei 公正 fair
kōsei na kyōsō 公正な競争 fair competition
kōsei-hōshū 公正報酬 fair return
kōsei-kyūfu 厚生給付 fringe benefit
kōsei-suru 構成するstructure *v.*
kōshi-kōzō 格子構造 grid structure
kōshikiteki-sutoraiki 公式的ストライキ official strike
kōshin 更新 update
kōshin-suru 更新する update *v.*
kōshō-chinginsa 交渉賃金差 wage drift
koshō-hakken-shūri 故障発見修理 trouble shooting
kōshō-senryaku 交渉戦略 negotiation strategy
kōshō-suru 交渉する nego-tiate *v.*
kōsoku-rosen 高速路線 fast track
kōtai-kyūjitsu 交代休日 staggered holidays
kōtaisei 交代制 shiftwork
kōtei-betsu-genka-keisan 工程別原価管理 process costing
kōtei-kanri 工程管理 process control
kōtei-keikaku-hiyō 工程計画費用 running expenses
kōtei-nagarezu 工程流れ図 flow line, flow process chart
kotei-hiyō 固定費用 fixed cost
kotei-kioku-sōchi 固定記憶装置 read-only memory (ROM)
kotei-shihon 固定資本 fixed capital
kotei-shisan 固定資産 fixed assets
kotei-shisan-baikyaku-zon 固定資産売却損 capital loss
koteihi 固定費 fixed costs
kouri-kakaku-shisū 小売価格指数 retail price index (RPI)
koyō 雇用 employment
koyō to kaiko 雇用と解雇 hiring and firing
koyō-jōken 雇用条件 conditions of employment
koyōkyoku 雇用局 employment bureau
kōzōteki-chinpuka 構造的陳腐化 built-in obsolescence
kujō-shori (-tetsuzuki) 苦情処理（手続き） grievance procedure
kumikomi 組み込み built-in
kumitate-rain 組立ライン assembly line
kunren 訓練 training
kunren-hitsuyō-bunseki 訓練必要分析 training needs analysis
kunren-hitsuyōsei-bunseki 訓練必要性分析 training needs analysis
kunren-nīzu-bunseki 訓練ニーズ分析 training needs analysis
kunren-shidōsha 訓練指導者 training officer
kunren-tantōsha 訓練担当者 training officer

kunrensei kaiten-ritsu 訓練生回転率 trainee turnover
kurikaeshi 繰り返し interactive
kurikaeshi-sagyō 繰り返し作業 interactive process
kuritikaru-pasu-bunseki クリティカルパス分析 critical path analysis (CPA)
kuritikaru-pasu-mesoddo クリティカル・パス・メソッド critical path method (CPM)
kurōzudo-shoppu クローズドショップ closed shop
kurōzudo-shoppu ni tsuika-kanyūsuru クローズドショップに追加加入する post-entry closed shop
kuwake-suru 区分けする compartmentalize *v.*
kyakuhon 脚本 scenario
kyoka o ete 許可を得て under licence
kyokuchi-tsūshinmō 局地通信網 local area network (LAN)
kyōdō-daihyōken 共同代表権 joint representation
kyōdō-keiei 共同経営 partnership
kyōdō-keieisha 共同経営者 partner
kyōdō-kettei 共同決定 co-determination
kyōdō-kōkoku 共同広告 corporate advertising
kyōdō-kumiai-shugi 協同組合主義 corporatism
kyōdō-sagyō 共同作業 synergy
kyōdō-shijō 共同市場 common market
kyōkō 恐慌 crash
kyōryokuteki 協力的 collaborative
kyōsō-jō no yūi 競争上の優位 competitive advantage
kyōsō-kakaku 競争価格 competitive price
kyōsō-kankei-bunseki 競争関係分析 competitor analysis
kyōsō-ryoku 競争力 ability to compete
kyōsō-nyūsatsu 競争入札 competitive tendering
kyōsō-senjutsu 競争戦術 competitive tactics
kyōsō-senryaku 競争戦略 competitive strategy
kyōsōsha-bunseki 競争者分析 competitor analysis
kyōsōteki 競争的 competitive
kyōsōteki-kakaku 競争的価格 competitive price
kyōsōteki-kōgeki 競争的攻撃 competitive thrust
kyōsōteki-senryaku 競争的戦略 competitive strategy
kyōsōteki-shigeki 競争的刺激 competitive stimulus
kyōsōteki-shisei 競争的姿勢 competitive position
kyōsōteki-taido 競争的態度 competitive position
kyōsōteki-yūi 競争的優位 competitive edge
kyōtei 協定 agreement
kyōtsū-tsūka 共通通貨 common currency
kyōtsūgo 共通語 common language
kyūka 休暇 holiday, day off
kyū-shī-sākuru キュー・シー・サークル quality circle
kyūryō no jōgen 給料の上限

wage ceiling
kyūshi-jikan 休止時間 down time
kyūtō 急騰 boom
kyūyo 給与 pay
kyūyo-jōshō-kyokusen 給与上昇曲線 salary progression curve
kyūyo-kikan 給与期間 pay round
kyūyo-kōjo 給与控除 payroll deduction
kyūyo-kōzō 給与構造 salary structure
kyūyo-minaoshi 給与見直し salary review
kyūyo-ruishin-kyokusen 給与累進曲線 salary progression curve
kyūyo-tōkyū 給与等級 salary grade
kyūyo-zei 給与税 payroll tax

M

mākettingu-mikkusu マーケッティングミックス marketing mix
mākettingu-yosan マーケッティング予算 marketing budget
machiawase-riron 待ち合わせ理論 queueing theory
maikuro-chippu マイクロ・チップ microchip
mainasu-shotoku-zei マイナス所得税 negative income tax
makuro マクロ macro
manējimento-baiauto マネージメント・バイアウト management buyout
manējimento-gēmu マネージメントゲーム management game
manējaru-guriddo マネージャルグリッド managerial grid
matorikkusu-kanri マトリックス管理 matrix management
matorikkusu-soshiki マトリックス組織 matrix organization
mattaku betsu no hanashi まったく別の話 different ball game
mausu (konpyūtā no shiji-kiki) マウス（コンピューターの指示機器） mouse
medama-shōhin 目玉商品 price-leader
media-bunseki メディア分析 media analysis
meirei-keitō 命令系統 chain of command, line of command
meisei-kakaku 名声価格 prestige pricing
meibo ni noseru 名簿に載せる shortlist *v.*
menkyo 免許 licence
miharinin 見張り人 picket
mijōjō-shōken 未上場証券 unlisted security
mijukurenkō 未熟練工 unskilled labour
mikaeri-torihiki 見返り取引 countertrade
mikomi-kaitō 見込回答 anticipatory response
mimaikin 見舞金 *ex gratia* payment
min'eika 民営化 privatization
min'eika-suru 民営化する privatize *v.*
minkan-kigyō 民間企業 private enterprise
mita-tōri 見たとおり WYSIWYG (What You See Is What You Get)
mitsumori-genka-sei 見積原価制 estimating systems costs
mitsumoru 見積る estimate *v.*
mijikai komāsharu-messēji 短いコマーシャルメッセージ subliminal advertising
mizumashi-koyō-yōkyū 水増し雇用要求 featherbedding
mochikabu 持ち株 shareholding
mochikabu-gaisha 持ち株会社 associate company, holding company
moderu モデル model
mogi-renshū 模擬練習 simulation
mogi-suru 模擬する simulate

v.

mojurā-seisan モジュラー生産 modular production

mojūru-sei モジュール性 modularity

mokei-soshiki 模型組織 matrix organization

mokuhyō 目標 target

mokuhyō ni hansuru tasseido 目標に反する達成度 performance against objectives

mokuhyō no yūsen-jun'i 目標の優先順位 hierarchy of goals

mokuhyō o settei-suru 目標を設定する target *v.*

mokuhyō-kakaku-settei 目標価格設定 target pricing

mokuhyō-kanri 目標管理 management by objectives (MBO)

mokuhyō-settei 目標設定 goal-setting, objective-setting, target-setting, targeting

mokuhyō-tansaku 目標探索 goal-seeking

mokuhyō-tassei 目標達成 goal-seeking

mokuhyō-kakaku 目標価格 target pricing

mokuteki 目的 objective

mokuteki ni hansuru tasseido 目的に反する達成度 performance against objectives

mokuteki no jun'i 目的の順位 hierarchy of goals

mondai-bunseki 問題分析 problem analysis

mondai-kaiketsu 問題解決 problem solving

mondai-kaiketsu ni tsuika-shishutsu suru 問題解決に追加支出する throw money at problems *v.*

mondai-ryōiki 問題領域 problem area

mondaiten 問題点 issue

morekuchi 漏れ口 leak

motodōri ni modosu 元どおりに戻す turn around *v.*

motokin 元金 seed money

mukei-shisan 無形資産 intangible assets, invisibles

mukekkan-undō 無欠陥運動 zero defects

mukō ni suru 無効にする bottom out *v.*

musakui-kansatsuhō 無作為観察法 random observation method

mushi-suru 無視する marginalize *v.*

N

nagare-keiro 流れ経路 flow line
nagare-sagyō-kōteizu 流れ作業工程図 flow process chart
nagare-sagyō-seisan 流れ作業生産 flow production
nagare-sagyōzu 流れ作業図 flow diagram
nagarezu 流れ図 flow chart
naibu-chōtatsu-suru 内部調達する internalize *v.*
naibu-kansa 内部監査 internal audit
naibu-ryūho 内部留保 retained profit
naibu-shūekiritsu 内部収益率 internal rate of return (IRR)
naiyō-kanrenzu 内容関連図 pertinence tree
nakagai-tesūryō 仲買手数料 brokerage fees
nakagainin 仲買人 broker
nan-chakuriku 軟着陸 soft landing
nanahikari-kōka 七光効果 halo effect
nanbāsu-gēmu ナンバース・ゲーム numbers game
nebiki 値引き price cutting
nebiki-suru 値引きする cut prices *v.*
negasa-kabu 値がさ株 blue-chip stock
nehaba 値幅 price range
nenji-hōkokusho 年次報告書 policy statement
nesage-suru 値下げする cut prices *v.*
nettowāku o tsukuru ネットワークを作る network *v.*
nettowāku-bunseki ネットワーク分析 network analysis
nettowāku-zukuri ネットワーク作り networking
nezumi-kyōsō 鼠競争 rat race
niage 荷揚げ mark-up
nichiyōhin 日用品 convenience goods
nijū-kazei-menjo 二重課税免除 double taxation relief
nijū-kyōkyūgen 二重供給源 dual sourcing
nikkahyō 日課表 pie chart
nikkin 日勤 day shift
nin'i-chūshutsuhō 任意抽出法 random sampling
nin'i-jikantai 任意時間帯 span of discretion
nin'i-kinmu-jikan 任意勤務時間 flexible working hours
ningen-kankei 人間関係 human relations
ningen-kōgaku 人間工学 human engineering, ergonomics
ninmu 任務 job assignment
ninshiki-suijun 認識水準 awareness level
nishinhō-sūji 二進法数字 bit (binary digit)
nīzu-bunseki ニーズ分析 needs analysis
nomi-ya ノミ屋 stag
nōhau ノウハウ know-how
nōki 納期 delivery time
nōritsu 能率 efficiency
nōritsu-kensa 能率検査 performance review
nōritsukyū 能率給 payment by result

nōryoku 能力 capability, ability
nōryoku-shiken 能力試験 aptitude test
nottori 乗っ取り take-over
nottoriya 乗っ取り屋 corporate raider
nyūryoku-sōchi 入力装置 computer input
nyūsha-go no kurōzudo-shoppu 入社後のクローズドショップ post entry closed shop

O

odayaka na hanbai 穏やかな販売 soft sell
odayaka na shōhō 穏やかな商法 soft sell
odayaka na urikomi 穏やかな売り込み soft selling
okiai 沖合 offshore
ōnā-keieisha オーナー経営者 owner manager
onrain オンライン on line
ōpun-shoppu オープンショップ open shop
ōshū-kyōdō-shijō 欧州共同市場 Euromarket
ōshū-kyōdōtai 欧州共同体 European Community (EC)
ōshū-tsūka-dōmei 欧州通貨同盟 European Monetary Union (EMU)
ōshū-tsūka-seido 欧州通貨制度 European Monetary System (EMS)
ōshū-tsūka-tan'i 欧州通貨単位 European Currency Unit (ECU)
ōtō-kigō 応答記号 answerback code
otori-shōhin おとり商品 loss-leader
otori-shōryaku おとり商略 leader merchandising
oya-gaisha 親会社 parent company

P

pātohō パート法 programme evaluation and review technique (PERT)
paramētā パラメーター parameter
parametarikku-keikaku パラメタリック計画 parametric programming
parametarikku-keikakuhō パラメタリック計画法 parametric programming
paretto-yusō パレット輸送 palletization
pasokon パソコン personal computer (PC)
projekuto o tsubusu プロジェクトをつぶす chunk a project *v.*
projekuto-hyōka プロジェクト評価 project assessment
puroguramu プログラム programme
puroguramingu プログラミング programming
puroguramu o sakusei-suru プログラムを作製する program *v.*
puroguramudo-gakushū プログラムド学習 programmed learning
purojekuto-bunseki プロジェクト分析 project analysis
purojekuto-chīmu プロジェクトチーム task force
purojekuto-hyōka プロジェクト評価 project assessment
purojekuto-kanri プロジェクト管理 project management
purojekuto-manējā プロジェクト・マネージャー project manager
purosesu o kioku-sōchi kara nozoku プロセスを記憶装置から除く roll out *v.*

R

rain to sutaffu ラインとスタッフ line and staff
rain-ashisutanto ラインアシスタント line assistant
rain-bumon no kanri ライン部門の管理 line management
rain-bumon no kanrisha ライン部門の管理者 line executive
rain-bumon no kantoku ライン部門の監督 line manager
rain-bumon no sekininsha ライン部門の責任者 line executive
rain-kanri ライン管理 line management
rain-kantokusha ライン監督者 line manager
rain-kengen ライン権限 line authority
rain-seisan ライン生産 line production
rain-soshiki ライン組織 line organization
raisensu-seisan o okonau ライセンス生産を行なう licence production *v.*
randamu-akusesu ランダムアクセス random access
rappu-toppu-shiki ラップトップ式 laptop
rappu-toppu-shiki-konpyūta ラップトップ式コンピュータ laptop computer
rebarejjido-baiauto レバレッジド・バイアウト leveraged buyout (LBO)
rebarejjido-biddo レバレッジド・ビッド leveraged bid
reigai-kanri 例外管理 management by exception
renketsu 連結 consolidation
renketsu-kaikei 連結会計 consolidated accounts
renketsu-kessan 連結決算 consolidated accounts
renzoku 連続 on stream
renzoku-nagare-sagyō-seisan 連続流れ作業生産 continuous-flow production
renzoku-zaikohin-shirabe 連続在庫品調べ continuous stocktaking
rēzā-purintā レーザープリンター laser printer
riaru-taimu リアルタイム real time
rieki 利益 profit
rieki ni taisuru eikyō 利益に対する影響 profit impact
rieki no haibun 利益の配分 profit sharing
rieki no kaizen 利益の改善 profit improvement
rieki no saitōshi 利益の再投資 ploughback
rieki o iji-suru 利益を維持する hold margins *v.*
rieki-haibun 利益配分 profit sharing
rieki-kaizen 利益改善 profit improvement
rieki-kōka 利益効果 profit impact
rieki-kyokudaika 利益極大化 profit maximization
rieki-mitōshi 利益見通し profit outlook
rieki-mokuhyō 利益目標 profit goal, profit target

rieki-senryaku 利益戦略 profit strategy
rieki-tan'i-bumon 利益単位部門 profit centre
rieki-tan'i-bumon-kaikei 利益単位部門会計 profit centre accounting
rieki-yōin-bunseki 利益要因分析 profit factor analysis
rīdingu-ejji リーディングエッジ leading edge
rijun 利潤 profit
rijun-bunpai-kyūyo 利潤分配給与 profit related pay
rijun-dōki 利潤動機 profit motive
rijun-keikaku 利潤計画 profit planning, profit projection
rijun-renkei-kyūyo 利潤連係給与 profit related pay
rijun-renrui 利潤連類 profit implication
rijun-saitekika 利潤最適化 profit optimization
rijun-yosō-bunseki 利潤予想分析 profit-factor analysis
rijun-zei 利潤税 profits tax
rinji no shigoto 臨時の仕事 jobbing
rinkai-keiro-bunseki 臨界経路分析 critical path analysis (CPA)
ririku 離陸 take off
ironteki 理論的 rational
robotto ロボット robot
robotto-kōgaku ロボット工学 robots
robottoka-suru ロボット化する robotize *v.*
rōdō 労働 labour
rōdō-kaitenritsu 労働回転率 labour turnover
rōdō-kankei 労働関係 labour relations
rōdō-kumiai (shokushu-betsu no) 労働組合（職種別の） trade union
rōdō-ryūdōsei 労働流動性 labour mobility
rōdō-saigai 労働災害 industrial injury
rōdō-shūyakuteki 労働集約的 labour intensive
rōdō-sōgi 労働争議 industrial dispute
rōdōryoku-chōtatsu (gen) 労働力調達（源） manpower resourcing
rōdōryoku-kanri 労働力管理 manpower management
rōdōryoku-yosō 労働力予想 manpower forecasting
rōdōsha 労働者 blue-collar worker, labourer
rōdōsha no kaitenritsu 労働者の回転率 labour turnover
rōdōsha-daihyō (sei) 労働者代表（制） worker representation
rōmuhi 労務費 labour costs
rōshi-funsō 労使紛争 labour dispute
rōshi-kankei 労使関係 industrial relations, labour relations
rōshi-kankeibu 労使関係部 industrial relations department
rōshi-kyōgi 労使協議 joint consultation
rōshi-kyōgikai 労使協議会 works council
rosu-mēkā ロスメーカー loss maker
rusuban-denwa 留守番電話 answerphone

ryakudatsusha 略奪者 predator
ryō 量 volume
ryūdō-fusai 流動負債 current liabilities
ryūdō-hiritsu 流動比率 current ratio
ryūdō-shihon 流動資本 circulating capital
ryūdō-shisan 流動資産 current assets, liquid assets
ryūdōsei-hiritsu 流動性比率 liquidity ratio
ryūtsū-channeru 流通チャンネル channels of distribution
ryūtsū-kanri 流通管理 distribution management
ryūtsū-keihi 流通経費 marketing appropriation, distribution costs
ryūtsū-keikaku 流通計画 distribution planning
ryūtsū-keiretsu 流通系列 chain of distribution
ryūtsū-keiro 流通経路 channels of distribution, distribution network, distribution channel
ryūtsū-keitō 流通系統 chain of distribution
ryūtsū-kikō 流通機構 distribution network
ryūtsū-seisaku 流通政策 distribution policy
ryūtsū-sekininsha 流通責任者 distribution manager

S

sabetsu(-taigū) 差別（待遇） discrimination
sabetsu-suru 差別する discriminate *v.*
sabetsu-tokusei (shōhin no) 差別特性（商品の） unique selling proposition (USP)
sabetsuka-suru 差別化する differentiate *v.*
sabetsuteki-kakaku 差別的価格 differential price
sabetsuteki-kakaku-seido 差別的価格制度 differential pricing
sabetsuteki-kakaku-settei 差別的価格設定 differential pricing
sabotāju サボタージュ go-slow
sage-sōba 下げ相場 down market
sagyō 作業 work, operations
sagyō no kanshi 作業の監視 performance monitoring
sagyō o kanshi-suru 作業を監視する monitor performance *v.*
sagyō-haibun 作業配分 dispatching
sagyō-hyōka 作業評価 performance review
sagyō-in 作業員 worker
sagyō-kanri 作業管理 operating management
sagyō-kanrisha 作業管理者 works manager, operations manager
sagyō-kanshi 作業監視 performance monitoring
sagyō-kantoku 作業監督 operations manager
sagyō-keikaku 作業計画 work schedule
sagyō-kenkyū 作業研究 work study
sagyō-kijun 作業基準 performance standard
sagyō-kōsei 作業構成 work structuring
sagyō-kōtei 作業工程 routing
sagyō-kōteizu 作業工程図 flow chart
sagyō-kōzōka 作業構造化 work structuring
sagyō-naiyō 作業内容 operations breakdown, work content
sagyō-nōryoku 作業能力 ergonometrics
sagyō-saikuru 作業サイクル work cycle
sagyō-shisū 作業指数 performance indicators
sagyō-sokutei 作業測定 work measurement
sagyō-tanjunka 作業単純化 work simplification
sagyō-tanmatsu 作業端末 work statement, work station
saiaku no shinario 最悪のシナリオ worst-case scenario
saibun 細分 subdivision, segmentation
saibunka 細分化 segmentation
sai-bunseki 再分析 variance analysis
saibunka-suru 細分化する segment *v.*

saichō-keiro-bunseki 最長経路分析 critical path analysis (CPA)
saidai-seihin-kachi 最大製品価値 maximum product value
saidaika-suru 最大化する maximize *v.*
saigai-taisaku 災害対策 contingency planning
saihaibi 再配備 redeployment
saihaichi-suru 再配置する redeploy *v.*
saihan-kakaku 再販価格 resale price
saihan-kakaku-iji-seido 再販価格維持制度 resale price maintenance (RPM)
saihensei 再編成 reorganization, restructuring
saihensei-suru 再編成する restructure *v.*
saikasseika-senryaku 再活性化戦略 reactive strategy
saiken 債券 bonds
saiken-kin'yū 債権金融 factoring
saikentō-suru 再検討する review *v.*
saikō-keiei-sekininsha 最高経営責任者 chief executive
saikō-keiei-sekininsha-seido 最高経営責任者制度 top management approach
saikō-keieisha 最高経営者 top management
saikōchiku 再構築 reconfiguration
saikunren 再訓練 retraining, booster training
saimu 債務 liabilities
saimu-hiritsu 債務比率 debt ratio
sainyū-saishutsu 歳入歳出 revenue expenditure (revex)
sairiyō 再利用 recycling
sairiyō-suru 再利用する recycle *v.*
saisan 採算 profit
saisenden-suru 再宣伝する re-image *v.*
saishin-kijitsu 最新期日 latest date
saishō-hiyō 最小費用 least-cost
saishutoku-genka 再取得原価 replacement costs
saishū-kekka 最終結果 bottom line
saishū-kijitsu 最終期日 latest date
saitei-chingin 最低賃金 minimum wage
saiteki-hatchūryō 最適発注量 economic order quantity
saiteki-seisanryō 最適生産量 economic manufacturing quantity
saiyō 採用 recruitment
saiyōji-tokubetsu-bōnasu 採用時特別ボーナス golden hello
sai-yūryō-kabu 最優良株 golden share
saizen no shinario 最善のシナリオ best-case scenario
sakimono-kawase-sōba 先物為替相場 forward exchange rate
sakimono-shijō 先物市場 forward market
sakimono-sōba 先物相場 forward rate
sakimono-suwappu 先物スワップ forward swap

sakimono-torihiki 先物取引 futures
sakuseishita yosan 作成した予算 prepared budget
sangyō-anzen 産業安全 industrial safety
sangyō-dantai 産業団体 trade association
sangyō-haikibutsu 産業廃棄物 industrial waste
sangyō-himitsu-hoji (-seido) 産業秘密保持（制度） industrial security
sangyō-katsudō 産業活動 industrial action
sangyō-kōgaku 産業工学 industrial engineering
sangyō-minshushugi 産業民主主義 industrial democracy
sangyō-saigai 産業災害 industrial injury
sangyō-shinri 産業心理 industrial psychology
sangyō-shinrigaku 産業心理学 industrial psychology
sangyō-supai 産業スパイ industrial espionage
sanka 参加 participation
sannyū-suru 参入する access, penetrate *v.*
sanpō 算法 algorithm
sanpuzu 散布図 scatter diagram
sanshutsu-yosan 産出予算 output budgeting
satei 査定 appraisal, assessment
satei-sentā 査定センター assessment centre
satei-suru 査定する appraise, assess *v.*
sayatori-gyōsha さや取り業者 arbitrageur
sayatori-kabu さや取り株 arbitrage stock
seichō-chiiki 成長地域 growth area
seichō-kanōsei 成長可能性 growth potential
seichō-sangyō 成長産業 growth industry
seichō-senryaku 成長戦略 growth strategy
seichō-shisū 成長指数 growth index
seido oyobi tetsuzuki 制度および手続き systems and procedures
seigen-kankō 制限慣行 restrictive practices (industrial)
seigyo-jōhō 制御情報 control information
seihin 製品 product
seihin no ryōiki 製品の領域 product area
seihin no saidai-kachi 製品の最大価値 maximum product value
seihin no tayōka 製品の多様化 product diversification
seihin no uchiage 製品の打ち上げ product launch
seihin o sabetsuka-suru 製品を差別化する product differentiate *v.*
seihin-bun'ya 製品分野 product range
seihin-bunpu 製品分布 product range
seihin-bunseki 製品分析 product analysis
seihin-chōsa 製品調査 product research
seihin-gainen 製品概念 product conception

seihin-genka 製品原価 cost of product
seihin-gurūpu 製品グループ product group
seihin-han'i 製品範囲 product area
seihin-ichiranhyō 製品一覧表 product portfolio
seihin-imēji 製品イメージ product image
seihin-jumyō 製品寿命 product life, product life-cycle
seihin-jumyō-yosoku 製品寿命予測 product life expectancy
seihin-kaihatsu 製品開発 product development
seihin-kairyō 製品改良 product improvement
seihin-kaizen 製品改善 product improvement
seihin-kanri 製品管理 product management
seihin-kanrisha 製品管理者 product manager
seihin-keikaku 製品計画 product planning
seihin-kensa 製品検査 product testing, product test
seihin-kōkoku 製品広告 product advertising
seihin-kōsei 製品構成 product mix
seihin-meisaihyō 製品明細表 product portfolio
seihin-sabetsuka 製品差別化 product differentiation
seihin-sabetsuka-suru 製品差別化する product differentiate *v.*
seihin-sagyō (-tasseido) 製品作業（達成度） product performance
seihin-seinō 製品性能 product performance
seihin-sekkei 製品設計 product design
seihin-senryaku 製品戦略 product strategy
seihin-shinraisei 製品信頼性 product reliability
seihin-shōkai 製品紹介 product profile
seihin-shūekiritsu 製品収益率 product profitability
seihin-tayōka 製品多様化 product diversification
seihinka-keikaku 製品化計画 product planning
seijuku-shijō 成熟市場 mature market
seikatsu-yōshiki 生活様式 lifestyle
seikeihi 生計費 cost of living
seinō-sokutei 性能測定 performance measurement
seisaku 政策 policy
seisan-buntan-keikaku 生産分担計画 share of production plan
seisan-chū 生産中 on stream
seisan-chūshi 生産中止 product abandonment
seisan-fukugōtai 生産複合体 production complex
seisan-genka 生産原価 cost of production
seisan-gijutsu 生産技術 production engineering
seisan-kachi 生産価値 break-up value
seisan-kanri 生産管理 manufacturing control,

production control, production management
seisan-kanrisha 生産管理者 production manager
seisan-keikaku 生産計画 production planning, production schedule
seisan-keikaku no buntan 生産計画の分担 share of production plan
seisan-keikaku oyobi kanri 生産計画および管理 production planning and control
seisan-keikaku-kanri 生産計画管理 production planning and control
seisan-keikaku-sakusei 生産計画策定 production scheduling
seisan-kijun 生産基準 production standard
seisan-kōgaku 生産工学 production engineering
seisan-kōtei 生産工程 production process
seisan-kōtei-shisetsu no haichi 生産工程施設の配置 process equipment layout
seisan-mokuhyō 生産目標 production targets
seisan-nōryoku 生産能力 manufacturing capacity, viability
seisan-nōryoku-riyō 生産能力利用 capacity utilization
seisan-rain 生産ライン product line
seisan-rikigaku 生産力学 product dynamics
seisan-sei 生産性 productivity
seisan-shisetsu no chingashi 生産施設の賃貸し plant hire
seisan-shisetsu-haichi-kenkyū 生産施設配置研究 plant layout study
seisan-shisetsu-sekkei 生産施設設計 process equipment layout
seisan-shisū 生産指数 production index
seisan-yotei 生産予定 production schedule
seisanbutsu-haiki 生産物廃棄 product abandonment
seisanhi 生産費 production costs
seisanjo 精算所 clearing house
seisansei 生産性 productivity
seisansei-kōjō-kōshō 生産性向上交渉 productivity bargaining
seisansei-kōjō-kyōtei 生産性向上協定 productivity arrangement
seisansei-kōjō-undō 生産性向上運動 productivity campaign, productivity drive
seisansei-kōshō 生産性交渉 productivity bargaining
seisansei-kyōtei 生産性協定 productivity agreement
seisansei-sokutei 生産性測定 productivity measurement
seisanteki-shisetsu-hozen 生産的施設保存 productive maintenance
seisanzai 生産財 industrial goods
seiseki-hyōka 成績評価 merit rating
seiteki-iyagarase 性的いやがらせ sexual harassment
seitō na hyōka 正当な評価 appreciation

seizō-kanri 製造管理 manufacturing control
seizō-kōtei 製造工程 production process
seizō-mokuhyō 製造目標 production target
seizō-nōryoku 製造能力 plant capacity
seizō-setsubi-haichi 製造設備配置 process equipment layout
seizō-suru 製造する manufacture *v.*
seisanteki-setsubi-hozen 生産的設備保全 productive maintenance
sekai-shijō 世界市場 global marketing
sekaika 世界化 globalization
sekaika-suru 世界化する globalize *v.*
sekaiteki-imēji 世界的イメージ global image
sekinin-buntan 責任分担 allocation of responsibilities
sekinin-kaikei 責任会計 responsibility accounting
sekinin-keitō 責任系統 linear responsibility
sekkei-gijutsu 設計技術 design engineering
sekkei-jimusho 設計事務所 design office
sekkeizu 設計図 blueprint
sekkyokuteki na katsudō 積極的な活動 go-getting
sekkyokuteki ni hataraku 積極的に働く hustle *v.*
sekkyokuteki-hanbetsu 積極的判別 positive discrimination
sekkyokuteki-sabetsu 積極的差別 positive discrimination
sen-kiroku 線記録 trade record
senden 宣伝 advertisement
senden-baitai 宣伝媒体 advertising media
senden-bun 宣伝文 advertising message
senden-hiyō 宣伝費用 advertising appropriation
senden-katsudō 宣伝活動 advertising drive, advertising campaign
senden-kōka 宣伝効果 advertising effectiveness
senden-sen 宣伝戦 advertising campaign
senden-shudai 宣伝主題 advertising theme
senden-tantōsha 宣伝担当者 advertising manager
senden-yosan 宣伝予算 advertising budget
senjutsuteki-keikaku 戦術的計画 tactical plan
senjutsuteki-kunren 戦術的訓練 tactical training
senkei-keikakuhō 線型計画法 linear programming
senken-yūsen-senryaku 先験優先戦略 proactive strategy
senkō-ōtō 先行応答 anticipatory response
senkuteki-seihin 先駆的製品 pioneer product
senmonka-keiei-shisutemu 専門家経営システム expert system
senmonka-komondan 専門家顧問団 brains trust
senmonka-seido 専門家制度 expert system
senmonka-yōsei 専門家養成 professionalization

senmu-torishimariyaku 専務取締役 executive director
senryaku 戦略 strategy
senryaku o tenkai-suru 戦略を展開する evolve strategy *v.*
senryaku-jisshi 戦略実施 strategy implementation
senryaku-keisei 戦略形成 strategy formulation
senryaku-suikō 戦略遂行 strategy implementation
senryakuteki dōmei (-kankei) 戦略的同盟（関係） strategic alliance
senryakuteki-bijinesu-tan'i 戦略的ビジネス単位 strategic business unit
senryakuteki-keikaku 戦略的計画 strategic planning
senryakuteki-sōgo-ison 戦略的相互依存 strategic interdependence
sensu o migaku センスを磨く sensitize *v.*
sentaku (fusei-na shikin no) 洗濯（不正な資金の），ロンダリング laundering
sentakuken-seido 選択権制度 option system
senzai-ishiki-kōkoku 潜在意識広告 subliminal advertising
senzai-seichōryoku 潜在成長力 growth potential
senzaiteki-kaite 潜在的買い手 potential buyer
sērusu-kabārejji セールスカバーレッジ sales coverage
setchi-hiyō 設置費用 set-up costs
setsubi-hi 設備費 cost of equipment
setsubi no chintai 設備の賃貸 equipment leasing
setsudan-ba 切断刃 cutting edge
setsuritsu-keikaku (-ritsuan) 設立計画（立案） organization planning
setsuritsu 設立 establishment
setsuritsu-hiyō 設立費用 start-up costs
shachō 社長 president
shagai 社外 out-house
shagai-chōtatsu 社外調達 outsourcing
shagai-jūyaku 社外重役 outside director
shagai-kigyō 社外企業 externalities
shain 社員 staff
shain no jisha-kaitori 社員の自社買取 worker buyout
shakai-bunkateki 社会文化的 socio-cultural
shakai-bunseki 社会分析 social analysis
shakai-hoshōhi 社会保障費 social security costs
shakai-keizai (gaku) 社会経済（学） socio-economic
shakai-shihon 社会資本 infrastructure
shanai 社内 in-house
shanai (teki) 社内（的） in-company
shanai-ryūho-riekikin 社内留保利益金 retained profits
shashu-keieisha 社主経営者 owner-manager
shayō-sangyō 斜陽産業 sunset industry
shiageru 仕上げる wind up *v.*
shichiya 質屋 pawn shop
shichōkaku-kizai 視聴覚機材

audio-visual aids
shidō-kijun 指導基準 guideline
shidōryoku 指導力 leadership
shidōsha 指導者 leader
shien-katsudō 支援活動 support activity
shigeki 刺激 incentive
shigen-haibun 資源配分 resource allocation
shigen-kanri 資源管理 resource management
shigen-kyōkyūgen (no kakuho) 資源供給源（の確保) sourcing
shigoto e no chōsen 仕事への挑戦 job challenge
shigoto no daishō 仕事の代償 job satisfaction
shigoto no jikkō 仕事の実行 job performance
shigoto no kinchō 仕事の緊張 work stress
shigoto no rieki 仕事の利益 job interest
shigoto no saikuru 仕事のサイクル work cycle
shigoto no shōraisei 仕事の将来性 job expectations
shigoto no sutoresu 仕事のストレス work stress
shigoto-nakama 仕事仲間 working party
shihainin 支配人 manager
shihainin no joshu 支配人の助手 assistant to manager
shihainin-dairi 支配人代理 deputy manager
shihaiteki-rieki 支配的利益 controlling interest
shihaiteki-riken 支配的利権 controlling interest
shiharai 支払 payment
shiharai-kijitsu 支払期日 due date
shiharai-shihon-satei 支払資本査定 capital expenditure appraisal
shiharau 支払う disburse *v.*
shihon ni kumiireru 資本に組み入れる capitalize *v.*
shihon no chikuseki 資本の蓄積 accumulation of capital
shihon-busoku 資本不足 capital rationing, under-capitalized
shihon-chōtatsu 資本調達 capital raising
shihon-datōsei 資本妥当性 capital adequacy
shihon-futaku 資本付託 capital commitment
shihon-hikiatekin 資本引当金 capital allowance
shihon-hoshōkin 資本保証金 capital allowance
shihon-itaku 資本委託 capital commitment
shihon-keikaku-hyōka 資本計画評価 capital project evaluation
shihon-keisei 資本形成 capital formation
shihon-keisū 資本係数 capital-output ratio
shihon-kōritsu 資本効率 return on capital employed (ROCE)
shihon-kōritsu 資本効率 return on capital
shihon-kōsei 資本構成 capital structure
shihon-kumiire 資本組み入れ capitalization

shihon-rimawari 資本利回り return on capital
shihon-satei 資本査定 capital appraisal
shihon-shishutsu 資本支出 capital expenditure (capex)
shihon-shishutsu-satei 資本支出査定 capital expenditure appraisal
shihon-shishutsu-yosan 資本支出予算 capital budget
shihon-shishutsu-yosan-hensei 資本支出予算編成 capital budgeting
shihon-shobun 資本処分 capital appreciation
shihon-shūyakuteki 資本集約的 capital-intensive
shihonteki-rieki 資本的利益 capital gain
shihonteki-rijun 資本的利潤 capital gain
shihonteki-sonshitsu 資本的損失 capital loss
shihonzai 資本財 capital goods
shihyō-sūji 指標数字 index number
shiire-buchō 仕入部長 purchasing manager
shiireru 仕入れる buy in *v.*
shiji (no) 支持（の） supportive
shijō de baibai-suru 市場で売買する market *v.*
shijō e no sannyū 市場への参入 market penetration
shijō no chikara 市場の力 market forces
shijō no ninshiki 市場の認識 market awareness
shijō no yosoku 市場の予測 market forecast
shijō o kaishimeru 市場を買い占める corner the market *v.*
shijō-binkansei 市場敏感性 market sensitive
shijō-chōsa 市場調査 market exploration, market survey, marketing research
shijō-dōkō 市場動向 market trend
shijō-dōtai-rikigaku 市場動態力学 market dynamics
shijō-gaiyō 市場概要 market profile
shijō-fuan 市場不安 market sensitive
shijō-hyōka 市場評価 market appraisal
shijō-ishiki 市場意識 market awareness
shijō-jikken 市場実験 market test
shijō (-himitsu) -jōhō 市場（秘密）情報 market intelligence
shijō-jōhō-ison 市場情報依存 market driven
shijō-kachi 市場価値 market value
shijō-kaihatsusha 市場開発者 market maker
shijō-kakaku 市場価格 market price
shijō-kakuzuke 市場格付け market rating
shijō-kanri 市場管理 market management
shijō-keikaku 市場計画 market plan
shijō-kenkyū 市場研究 market study
shijō-kensa 市場検査 market test

shijō-kinri 市場金利 market rating
shijō-kōzō 市場構造 market structure
shijō-kubun 市場区分 market segments
shijō-purofīru 市場プロフィール market profile
shijō-rikigaku 市場力学 market dynamics
shijō-saibunka 市場細分化 market segmentation
shijō-sannyū 市場参入 market penetration
shijō-satei 市場査定 market appraisal
shijō-sen'yūritsu 市場占有率 market share
shijō-senryaku 市場戦略 marketing strategy
shijō-senzairyoku 市場潜在力 market potential
shijō-shintō (hōhō) 市場浸透（方法） market saturation
shijō-shintō-kakaku (seisaku) 市場浸透価格（政策） penetration pricing
shijō-tenbō 市場展望 market prospect
shijō-torihiki 市場取引 marketing
shijō-unyō 市場運用 marketing appropriation
shijō-yosoku 市場予測 market force
shijōsei no aru 市場性のある marketable
shikakehin 仕掛け品 work in progress
shikaku 視覚 vision
shikaku-shisa-suru 視覚示唆する screen *v.*
shiken-hanbai 試験販売 test marketing
shikenteki-seisan 試験的生産 pilot production
shiki 指揮 lead
shikin o kyōkyū-suru 資金を供給する finance *v.*
shikin-chōtatsu 資金調達 capital raising
shikin-furō 資金フロー funds flow
shikin-guri 資金操り cash flow
shikin-un'yōhyō 資金運用表 source and disposition of funds
shimekiri-bi 締め切り日 deadline
shindan-tejun 診断手順 diagnostic routine
shindo-bunseki 深度分析 depth analysis
shindo-kanri(seisan-kōtei no) 進度管理（生産工程の） progress control
shinhakkō-shōken no uridashi 新発行証券の売り出し flotation
shinkabu-hikiukeken-nyūsatsu 新株引受権入札 pre-emptive bid
shinki-saiyō-suru 新規採用する recruit *v.*
shinkō-chū no 進行中の on-going
shinkō-chū no shigoto 進行中の仕事 work in progress
shinkō-sangyō-koku 新興産業国 newly industrialized country (NIC)
shinkoku 申告 declaration
shinku-tanku シンクタンク think tank

shinpojiumu シンポジウム symposium
shinraido 信頼度 reliability
shinri-shiken 心理試験 psychometric testing
shinri-sokutei-shiken 心理測定試験 psychometric testing
shinriteki-kakaku 心理的価格 psychological pricing
shinriteki-kakaku-settei 心理的価格設定 psychological pricing
shinseihin no uridashi 新製品の売り出し product launch
shinseihin-kaihatsu 新製品開発 new product development
shinshi-kyōtei 紳士協定 gentleman's agreement
shinsō-mensetsuhō 深層面接法 depth interview
shin'yō-kakuzuke 信用格付け credit rating
shin'yō-kanri 信用管理 credit control, credit management
shiryō 資料 materials
shiryō-shūshū 資料収集 data gathering
shisaku 試作 pilot production
shisakuhin 試作品 pioneer products
shisan 資産 assets
shisan 試算 test calculation
shisan-fusai-kanri 資産負債管理 asset liability management
shisan-hakudatsu 資産はく奪 asset-stripping
shisan-hōshutsu 資産放出 asset-stripping
shisan-kachi 資産価値 asset value
shisan-kaiten (ritsu) 資産回転（率） asset turnover
shisan-kanri 資産管理 portfolio management, asset management
shisan-meisaihyō 資産明細表 asset portfolio
shisan-saihyōka 資産再評価 revaluation of assets
shisan-sentaku 資産選択 portfolio selection
shisan-shūeki 資産収益 earnings on assets
shisetsu-chintai (-keiyaku) 施設賃貸（契約） equipment leasing
shisetsu-nōryoku 施設能力 plant capacity
shisetsu-riyōdo 施設利用度 capacity utilization
shisha 支社 branch office
shisutemu システム system
shisutemu-apurōchi システムアプローチ systems approach
shisutemu-bunseki システム分析 systems analysis
shisutemu-enjinia システム・エンジニア systems engineer
shisutemu-genka-mitsumori システム原価見積 estimating systems costs
shisutemu-ka-shita システム化した systematized
shisutemu-kanri システム管理 systems management
shisutemu-kanri-kigyō システム管理企業 system-managed company
shisutemu-keikaku システム計画 systems planning
shisutemu-kōgaku システム工学 systems engineering

shisutemu-riron システム理論 systems theory
shisutemu-sekkei システム設計 systems design
shisutemu-shorihō システム処理法 systems approach
shisū-dōkō 指数動向 exponential trend
shisū-heikatsuhō 指数平滑法 exponential smoothing
shita kara no iken-gushin 下からの意見具申 bottom-up
shitauke 下請け subcontracting
shitauke-gaisha 下請け会社 subsidiary company
shitauke-gyōsha 下請け業者 subcontractor
shitauke-keiyaku o suru 下請け契約をする subcontract *v.*
shiten 支店 branch
shiunten 試運転 field testing, test run
shiyō-kanō-jikan 使用可能時間 uptime (comp.)
shiyō-kikan 使用期間 use-by date
shiyō-shihon-gaku 使用資本額 capital employed
shiyō-shihon-kōritsu 使用資本効率 return on capital employed (ROCE)
shiyōsha no taido 使用者の態度 user attitude
shizen-sonmō 自然損耗 natural wastage
shōbai 商売 quotient
shōdan 商談 sales talk
shōdō 衝動 impulse
shōdō-gai 衝動買い impulse buying
shōdō-gai-shōhin 衝動買い商品 impulse goods
shōdō-uri 衝動売り impulse sales
shōgai 障害 bottleneck
shōgyō-ginkō 商業銀行 commercial bank, merchant bank
shōhi-busshi 消費物資 consumer goods
shōhin 商品 commodity
shōhin-shijō 商品市場 commodity market
shōhin-shurui-seiri 商品種類整理 variety reduction
shōhin-torihiki 商品取引 commodity exchange
shōhinka-suru 商品化する commoditize *v.*
shōhisha no shūchūsei 消費者の集中性 consumer convergence
shōhisha no taido 消費者の態度 user attitude
shōhisha-baishō 消費者賠償 consumer satisfaction
shōhisha-bukka-shisū 消費者物価指数 consumer price index
shōhisha-chōsa 消費者調査 consumer research
shōhisha-hannō 消費者反応 consumer-responsive
shōhisha-hogo 消費者保護 consumer protection
shōhisha-kakaku-shisū 消費者価格指数 consumer price index
shōhisha-katsudō 消費者活動 consumerism
shōhisha-kōdō 消費者行動 consumer behaviour
shōhisha-manzoku 消費者満足 consumer satisfaction
shōhisha-meibo 消費者名簿

consumers' list
shōhisha-paneru 消費者パネル consumers' panel
shōhisha-shūgō 消費者集合 consumer convergence
shōhisha-teikō 消費者抵抗 consumer resistance
shōhizai 消費財 consumer goods
shōhyō no yūkō-han'i 商標の有効範囲 brand stretching
shōhyō-ninshikido 商標認識度 brand recognition
shōiki-bōei 商域防衛 turf protection
shōken 商圏 trading area
shōken-hogo 商権保護 turf protection
shōkenka 証券化 securitization
shōkenka-suru 証券化する securitize *v.*
shōken-shijō 証券市場 stock market
shōkokin 証拠金 profit margin
shōkokin-ritsu 証拠金率 cover ratio
shokkai 職階 job classification
shokuba 職場 workplace
shokuba-gai-kunren 職場外訓練 off-the-job training
shokuba-hōki 職場放棄 walkout
shokuba-iinkai 職場委員会 works committee
shokubagai-kunren 職場外訓練 off-the-job training
shokubanai-kunren 職場内訓練 training within industry (TWI)
shokugyō-kunren 職業訓練 vocational training
shokugyō-shidō 職業指導 vocational guidance
shokugyōjō no kiken 職業上の危険 occupational hazard
shokuin(-saiyō)-keikaku 職員（採用）計画 staff planning
shokuin-hyōka 職員評価 staff appraisal
shokuin-idō 職員移動 staff mobility
shokuin-kanri 職員管理 staff management
shokuin-kansa 職員監査 staff audit
shokuin-kyōkyū 職員供給 staff resourcing
shokuin-mitōshi 職員見通し staff forecasting
shokuin-shokumu 職員職務 staff commitment
shokuin-soshiki 職員組織 staff organization
shokumu 職務 job assignment
shokumu no kaizen 職務の改善 job improvement
shokumu no manzokudo 職務の満足度 job satisfaction
shokumu no tanjunka 職務の単純化 job simplification
shokumu-bunrui 職務分類 job classification
shokumu-bunseki 職務分析 job analysis
shokumu-buntan 職務分担 job sharing
shokumu-hōshū 職務報酬 job compensation
shokumu-hoshō 職務保証 job security
shokumu-ichiran(-hyō) 職務一覧（表） role set
shokumu-jūjitsu 職務充実

job enrichment
shokumu-kakudai 職務拡大 job enlargement
shokumu-kanri 職務管理 functional management
shokumu-ken'eki 職務権益 job interest
shokumu-kijutsusho 職務記述書 job description
shokumu-kyōka 職務強化 job enhancement
shokumu-meisaisho 職務明細書 job specification
shokumu-satei 職務査定 job evaluation
shokumu-sekinin 職務責任 functional responsibility
shokumu-sekinin(sei) 職務責任（制） linear responsibility
shokumu-sekkei 職務設計 job design
shokumu-setsumei 職務説明 job portfolio
shokumu-suikō 職務遂行 job performance
shokumujō no kitai 職務上の期待 job expectations
shokunō-kankei 職能関係 functional relations
shokunō-kyū 職能給 wages based on job evaluation
shokunō-soshiki 職能組織 functional organization
shōmi-genka 正味現価 net present value (NPV)
shōmi-ryūdō-shisan 正味流動資産 net current assets
shōmōhin 消耗品 consumables
shōraisei 将来性 feasiblity
shōrei-keikaku 奨励計画 incentive scheme
shōrei-seido 奨励制度 incentive scheme
shori-nōryoku 処理能力 throughput
shōsai na intabyū 詳細なインタビュー in-depth interview
shōshin 昇進 promotion (personnel)
shōshin no 昇進の promotional
shōshin-seisaku 昇進政策 promotional policy
shōshūdan-zukuri 小集団作り team building
shōsū (ha) no rieki 少数（派）の利益 minority interest
shōten 焦点 focus
shōten o awaseru 焦点を合わせる focus *v.*
shotoku 所得 income
shotoku-zei 所得税 income tax
shōyo 賞与 bonus
shōyo-an 賞与案 bonus scheme
shōyo-seido 賞与制度 bonus scheme
shoyūken-hakudatsu 所有権はく奪 divestment
shudan 手段 mean
shudō-kabu 主導株 market leader
shūnyū 収入 income
shutoku 取得 acquisition
shutoku-jōkyō 取得状況 acquisition profile
shutoku-seiseki 取得成績 acquisition profile
shutsuryoku 出力 output
shutsuryoku-sōchi 出力装置 computer output
shūchū-seisan 集中生産

intensive production
shūchūka 集中化 centralization
shūchūka-suru 集中化する centralize *v.*
shūdan-kanri 集団管理 batch control
shūdan-rikigaku 集団力学 group dynamics, methectics
shūeki 収益 earnings yield
shūeki-gaku 収益額 earnings yield
shūeki-gyōseki 収益業績 earnings performance
shūeki-ritsu 収益率 rate of return
shūeki-shisan 収益資産 earnings on assets
shūekiryoku 収益力 earning power
shūekisei 収益性 profitability
shūekisei-bunseki 収益性分析 profitability analysis
shūekiteki-shishutsu 収益的支出 revenue expenditure (revex)
shūhen-shijō 周辺市場 fringe market
shūhen-sōchi 周辺装置 peripheral equipment, peripherals
shūjuku-kyokusen 習熟曲線 learning curve
shūsen-ryō 周旋料 brokerage
shuyō-kai-yōin 主要買い要因 key buying factors
shuyō-kanriten-ichiranhyō 主要管理点一覧表 milestone chart
shuyō-seikō-yōin 主要成功要因 key success factors
sōdairiten 総代理店 sole agent
sōdan-suru 相談する consult *v.*
sofutouea ソフトウエア software
sofutouea-enjinia ソフトウエア・エンジニア software engineer
sofutouea-gaisha ソフトウエア会社 software firm
sofutouea-hanbai-gyōsha ソフトウエア販売業者 software broker
sofutouea-nakagaigyō ソフトウエア仲買業 software broker
sofutouea-tekiyō-gyōmu ソフトウエア適用業務 software application
sofutouea-gijutsusha ソフトウエア技術者 software engineer
sofutouea-pakkēji ソフトウエア・パッケージ software package
sofutouea-shisutemu ソフトウエア・システム software system
sōgo-fujo 相互扶助 synergism
sōgo-hyōka 相互評価 mutual recognition
sōgo-ninshiki 相互認識 mutual recognition
sōgo-rikai o samatageru mono 相互理解を妨げるもの Chinese wall
sōgo-tokkyo-shiyōken 相互特許使用権 cross-licensing
sōgō-puroguramu 総合プログラム programme package
sōgō-purojekuto-kanri 総合プロジェクト管理 integrated project management

sōgō-zaimuhyō 総合財務表 group accounts
sōgōteki-hinshitsu 総合的品質 total quality
sōgōteki-kōjō-hozen 総合的工場保全 total plant maintenance
sōgōteki-purojekuto-kanri 総合的プロジェクト管理 integrated project management (IPM)
sōgyō-teishi 操業停止 shut-down
sōkan-kankei 相関関係 correlation
sōkatsu-kanjō 総括勘定 group accounts
sōkatsu-kanri 総括管理 general management
sōkeihi-kachi-bunseki 総経費価値分析 overhead value analysis (OVA)
sōki-intai 早期引退 early retirement
sōki-teinen 早期定年 early retirement
sōkin-hōhō 送金方法 remittance policy
sōkin-hōshin 送金方針 remittance policy
sokketsu-kyakka 即決却下 summary dismissal
sōko-gyōmu 倉庫業務 warehousing
sokudo 速度 bring up to speed *v.*
sokuji-kettei 即時決定 quick fix
sokushahō 速射法 quick-fire (situation)
sokutei-kijun 測定基準 benchmark
son'eki-bunki-bunseki 損益分岐分析 break-even analysis
son'eki-bunki-ryō 損益分岐量 break-even quantity
son'eki-bunkiten 損益分岐点 breakdown point
son'eki-bunseki 損益分析 cost-volume-profit analysis
son'eki-keisansho 損益計算書 statement of profits and losses
son'eki-nashi no hanbai 損益無しの販売 break-even sales
songai 損害 damage, loss
songai-baishō 損害賠償 compensation for damage
songai-baishō-kigen 損害賠償期限 damage limitation
songai-gentei-renshū 損害限定練習 damage limitation exercise
songai-hoken 損害保険 accident insurance
sonshitsu o sakugen-suru 損失を削減する cut one's losses *v.*
sōrieki 総利益 gross margin, gross profit
sōrijun 総利潤 gross profit
sōsa-kanō na 操作可能な operational
sōsai-rōn 相殺ローン back-to-back loans
soshiki 組織 organization
soshiki no ichiin 組織の一員 team player
soshiki-bunka 組織文化 organization culture
soshiki-keikaku(-sakutei) 組織計画（策定） organization planning
soshiki-kiroku 組織記録

organigram
soshiki-kōsei 組織構成 organization structure
soshiki-riron 組織理論 organization theory
soshiki-yoyū 組織余裕 organizational slack
soshikika-suru 組織化する systematize *v.*
soshikinai-keitōzu 組織内系統図 pertinence tree
soshikiteki na fushin 組織的な不振 organizational slack
soshikiteki na hatten 組織的な発展 organizational development
soshikiteki na henkō 組織的な変更 organizational change
soshikiteki na yūkōsei 組織的な有効性 organizational effectiveness
soshikiteki-kōdō 組織的行動 organizational behaviour
soshikiteki-kōka 組織的効果 organizational effectiveness
soshikizu 組織図 organization chart
soshō no taishō to naru 訴訟の対象となる actionable
sōshō 総称 generic
sōzoku-keikaku 相続計画 succession planning
sōzō-kanjō 創造勘定 creative accounting
sōzōteki-shijō 創造的市場 creative marketing
sōzōteki-shikō 創造的思考 creative thinking
sūchi-seigyo 数値制御 numerical control
sūgakuteki-keikakuhō 数学的計画法 mathematical programming
suichoku-gappei 垂直合併 vertical integration
suihei-shikō 水平思考 lateral thinking
suihei-undōjō 水平運動場 level playing field
suiheiteki-gappei 水平的合併 horizontal integration
suisoku-suru 推測する guesstimate *v.*
suisokuteki-kettei 推測的決定 guesstimate
suitchi-torēdingu スイッチトレーディング switch trading
sūji o sōsa-suru 数字を操作する massage the figures *v.*
sukui no kami 救いの神 white knight
supeinteki-kanshū スペイン的慣習 Spanish practices
superu-chekku スペルチェック spellcheck
supin-ofu-kōka スピンオフ効果 spin-off effects
suraidingu-sukēru スライディング・スケール sliding scale
suraido-sei スライド制 sliding scale
sūri-keikakuhō 数理計画法 mathematical programming
sutaffu-ashisutanto スタッフアシスタント staff assistant
sutaffu-soshiki スタッフ組織 staff organization
suto-kinshi-jōkō スト禁止条項 no-strike clause
suto-yaburi スト破り blackleg, scab
sutoraiki o suru ストライキをする strike *v.*

sutoraiki-kinshi-jōkō ストライキ禁止条項 no-strike clause

suwarikomi-sutoraiki 座り込みストライキ sit-down strike

T

T-gurūpu-kunren ティーグループ訓練 T-group training
tān-araundo-taimu ターンアラウンドタイム turnaround time
tachiagari-kukan 立ち上がり区間 leading edge
tai-shiyōsha-senryaku 対使用者戦略 user strategy
taido-chōsa 態度調査 attitude survey
taido-chōsei 態度調整 positioning
taigai-kankei 対外関係 external relations
taiken no kikitori 体験の聞き取り debriefing
taikyū-shōhizai 耐久消費財 consumer durables
taikyūzai 耐久財 durables, durable goods
taiō-tsūka 対応通貨 parallel currency
tairyō-seisan 大量生産 mass production
taishaku-taishōhyō 貸借対照表 balance sheet
taishaku-taishōhyō-kansa 貸借対照表監査 balance sheet auditing
taishoku 退職 retirement
taishokukin 退職金 severance pay
taishō o shibotta eigyō 対象をしぼった営業 niche marketing
taiwashiki 対話式 interactive
tajū-kaiki-bunseki 多重回帰分析 multiple regression analysis (MRA)
tajū-media-kunren 多重メディア訓練 multimedia training
tajū-shori 多重処理 multi-access
takaku-keiei 多角経営 multiple management
takakuka-senryaku 多角化戦略 diversification strategy
takane o tsukeru 高値を付ける overprice *v.*
takanekabu 高値株 high flier
takujōgata 卓上型 desktop
takujōgata-konpyūta 卓上型コンピュータ desktop computer
takumashii たくましい robust
tan'itsu-kyōkyūgen 単一供給源 single sourcing
tan'itsu-shijō 単一市場 single market
tan'itsu-tsūka 単一通貨 single currency
tanjun-sagyō-kōjō 単純作業工場 screwdriver factory
tanki-keikaku 短期計画 short-term planning
tankiteki-hōhō 短期的方法 short-term method
tanki-yūshi 短期融資 call loan
tanmatsu (-sōchi) 端末（装置） terminal
tanpo 担保 collateral
tanpo-shōken 担保証券 collateral security
tansaku-hōhō 探索方法

heuristics
tansaku-suru 探索する explore *v.*
tantaihō 単体法 simplex method
tasseido-satei 達成度査定 performance rating
tasuku-fōsu タスクフォース task force
tasū (-ha) no rieki 多数（派）の利益 majority interest
tayō na dentatsu-shudan no kunren 多様な伝達手段の訓練 multimedia training
tayōka 多様化 diversification
tayōka-senryaku 多様化戦略 diversification strategy
tayōka-suru 多様化する diversify *v.*
tedori-chingin 手取り賃金 take-home pay
tedori-kyūryō 手取り給料 take-home pay
teian 提案 proposal
teian-seido 提案制度 suggestion scheme
teigijutsu 低技術 low-tech
teiin-satei 定員査定 staff inspection
teikaihatsu-koku 低開発国 less developed country (LDC)
teikakaku-kabu 低価格株 low flier
teikakaku-shōhin 低価格商品 low-cost commodity
teikisen-keikaku 定期船計画 linear programming
teikiteki-hoshu 定期的保守 preventive maintenance
tekiōsei no aru kigyō 適応性のある企業 flexible firm
tekiōsei-kanri 適応性管理 adaptive control
tekisei-hōshū 適正報酬 fair return
tekisei-rijun 適性利潤 reasonable profit
tekisei-shiken 適性試験 aptitude test
teko no sayō テコの作用 leverage
tenkaihyō 展開表 spreadsheet
tenkan-shasai 転換社債 loan stock
tenken-suru 点検する verify *v.*
tensū-hyōkahō 点数評価法 points-rating method
tesūryō 手数料 premium
tesūryō o toru 手数料を取る hold margins *v.*
tetsuzuki 手続き procedure
tetsuzuki-jō no 手続き上の procedural
tī-gurūpu-kunren Tグループ訓練 T-group training
tojita-rūpu 閉じたループ closed loop
tokkyo(-ken) 特許（権） patent
tokkyo-baibai 特許売買 patent trading
tokkyo-bōeki 特許貿易 patent trading
tokkyo-shiyōryō 特許使用料 royalty
tokkyo-shutsugan 特許出願 patent application
tokkyoken-shingai 特許権侵害 piracy
tokuisaki 得意先 purchaser
tokutei no seikatsu-yōshiki o

taishō tosita kōkoku 特定の生活様式を対象とした広告 lifestyle packaging

tomobataraki de kodomo no nai fūfu 共働きで子供のない夫婦 dinkie, dink

tōgō-hinshitsu-kanri 統合品質管理 total quality control (TQC), total quality management (TQM)

tōgō-keiei-shisutemu 統合経営システム integrated management system

tōgō-kei'ei-soshiki 統合経営組織 integrated management system

tōgō-keikaku-kanri 統合計画管理 integrated project management

tōgō-pakkēji 統合パッケージ integrated package

tōgō-purojekuto-kanri 統合プロジェクト管理 integrated project management (IPM)

tōgō-suru 統合する integrate *v.*

tōgōka 統合化 integration

tōgōteki-hinshitsu-kanri 統合的品質管理 total quality control (TQC), total quality management (TQM)

tōgōteki-keiei-jōhō-kanri-seido 統合的経営情報管理制度 integrated management system

tōgōteki-kōjō-hoshu 統合的工場保守 total plant maintenance

tōkei-chōsa 統計調査 desk research

tōkei-hyō 統計表 statistical table

tōkei-hyōhon 統計標本 statistical sampling

tōkeiteki-hyōhon-chūshutsu 統計的標本抽出 statistical sampling

tōkeiteki-kanri 統計的管理 statistical control

tōketsu-suru 凍結する freeze *v.*

tōnyū-sanshutsu-bunseki 投入産出分析 input-output analysis

tōnyū-sanshutsuhyō 投入産出表 input-output table

tōnyūguchi 投入口 slot

tōroku-shōhyō 登録商標 registered trademark

tōshi 投資 investment

tōshi kara no shūeki 投資からの収益 return on investment

tōshi-bunseki 投資分析 investment analysis

tōshi-busoku 投資不足 disinvestment

tōshi-genzei 投資減税 investment tax credit

tōshi-ginkō 投資銀行 investment bank

tōshi-hōshin 投資方針 investment policy

tōshi-hyōka 投資評価 investment appraisal

tōshi-ka 投資家 investor

tōshi-kanri 投資管理 investment management

tōshi-keikaku 投資計画 investment programme

tōshi-keikaku-hyōka 投資計画評価 capital project evaluation

tōshi-kijun 投資基準 investment criteria
tōshi-kōritsu 投資効率 return on investment
tōshi-mikkusu 投資ミックス investment mix
tōshi-puroguramu 投資プログラム investment programme
tōshi-satei 投資査定 investment appraisal
tōshi-seisaku 投資政策 investment policy
tōshi-shikin 投資資金 stake
tōshi-yosan 投資予算 investment budget
tōshizai 投資財 investment goods
tōsoku-yobidashi-kioku-sōchi 等速呼び出し記憶装置 random access memory (RAM)
tōza-shisan 当座資産 quick assets
toppa 突破 breakthrough
toraburu o kaiketsu-suru kinkyūsochi トラブルを解決する緊急措置 fire fighting
torakku-rekōdo トラック・レコード track record
torihiki 取引 deal
torihiki ga seiritsu-suru 取り引きが成立する reach a deal *v.*
torihiki-bunseki 取り引き分析 transactional analysis (TA)
torihiki-chiiki 取引地域 trading area
torihiki-jō no 取引上の transactional
torihiki-kankei 取引関係 business relations
torihiki-keikaku 取引計画 trading programme
torihiki-kikai 取引機会 market opportunity
torihiki-seigen 取引制限 restrictive practices
torihiki-yosoku 取引予測 market prospects
torikkuru-daun-riron トリックル・ダウン理論 trickle-down theory
torishimariyaku 取締役 director
torishimariyaku-kai 取締役会 board meeting
torishimariyakukai ni yoru kanri 取締役会による管理 board control
tsubusu (keikaku o-) 潰す（計画を） crash *v.*
tsuika-shisetsu 追加施設 add-on equipment
tsuiseki-chōsa 追跡調査 follow-up
tsuiseki-suru 追跡する follow up *v.*
tsunagi-babai つなぎ売買 hedging
tsunagi-sōsa つなぎ操作 hedging operations
tsunagi-uri-suru つなぎ売りする hedge *v.*
tsūjō-unten 通常運転 hacking
tsūka-kyōkyū(ryō) 通貨供給（量） money supply
tsūshin-channeru 通信チャンネル channels of communication
tsūshin-hanbai 通信販売 mail order
tsūshin-kyōiku (ni yoru gakushū) 通信教育（による

学習） open learning
tsūshin-riron 通信理論
communications theory
tsūshinmō 通信網
communications network
tsuyokisuji 強気筋 bull

U

uchiage 打ち上げ launch
uchikiri-gendo 打ち切り限度 cut-off point
uinchesutā-disuku ウインチェスターディスク Winchester disk
uirusu ウイルス virus
ukai-suru 迂回する bypass *v.*
ukeoi-shigoto 請負仕事 piecework
un'ei-kanri-hōshiki 運営管理方式 administrative control procedure
un'yu 運輸 transportation
unmei-kanshinin 運命監視人 doomwatcher
unpan 運搬 materials handling
unpan-kanri 運搬管理 materials handling
unten-keihi 運転経費 running expenses
unten-shikin 運転資金 working capital
uri-sōba 売り相場 bear market
uriage-bunseki 売上分析 sales analysis
uriage-kitai 売上期待 sales expectations
uriage-mitsumori 売上見積 sales estimate
uriagedaka 売上高 sales volume
uriagedaka-bunseki 売上高分析 sales analysis
uriagedaka-genkai-rieki-ritsu 売上高限界利益率 profit-volume ratio (P/V)
uriagehin-kōsei 売上品構成 sales mix
uriageryō-hiritsu 売上量比率 profit-volume ratio (P/V)
uridasu 売り出す tender *v.*
uriharau 売り払う trade off *v.*
urikakekin-saiken-kaitori 売掛金債権買取 factoring
urite-shijō 売り手市場 sellers' market
urite-sōba 売り手相場 bear market
uritsukusu 売り尽くす sell out *v.*
utagawashii kakaku (no chōsa) 疑わしい価格（の調査） blue-sky (research)
utagawashii-torihiki 疑わしい取り引き grey market

W

wakai-suru 和解する conciliate *v.*
wāpuro ワープロ word processor (WP)
wariateru 割り当てる apportion *v.*, appropriate *v.*
warifuru 割り振る allocate *v.*
warimashi-shōyo 割増賞与 premium bonus
warui-men 悪い面 downside

Y

yakin 夜勤 night shift
yakuin 役員 director
yakuin-hōshū 役員報酬 executive compensation
yamaneko-suto(raiki) 山猫スト（ライキ） wildcat strike
yappī ヤッピー yuppie
yarinaoshi-suru やり直しする rerun *v.*
yasune o tsukeru 安値を付ける underprice *v.*
yatou 雇う hire *v.*
yobi-mizu (seisaku) 呼び水（政策） pump priming
yobi-seisan-nōryoku 予備生産能力 spare capacity
yoku junbi-sareta よく準備された well-packaged
yōshiki 様式 mode
yōso 要素 factor
yōten-ha'aku 要点把握 scanning
yosan 予算 budget
yosan no wariate 予算の割当 budget appropriation
yosan no yosoku 予算の予測 budget forecasting
yosan o kumu 予算を組む budget *v.*
yosan-haibun 予算配分 budget allotment
yosan-hensei 予算編成 budgeting
yosan-hensei-kanri 予算編成管理 budgeting control
yosan-kanri 予算管理 budgetary control
yosan-kijun 予算基準 budget standard
yosan-mitooshi 予算見通し budget forecast
yosan-seigen 予算制限 budget constraint
yosan-wariate 予算割当 budget appropriation
yosan-yosoku 予算予測 budget forecasting
yosanteki-seiyaku 予算的制約 budget constraint
yosoku 予測 forecast, forecasting
yosō 予想 second guessing
yosō-suru 予想する second guess *v.*
yotei o tateru 予定を立てる schedule *v.*
yotei (-sakusei) 予定（作成） scheduling
yotei (-hyō) 予定（表） schedule
yotei-dōsa-jikan-hōshiki 予定時間動作方式 predetermined motion and time system (PMTS)
yotei-kijitsu 予定期日 expected date
yowakisuji 弱気筋 bear
yunyū 輸入 import
yutaka na temoto-ryūdōsei 豊かな手元流動性 cash-rich
yūbin 郵便 mail
yūbin no shurui-betsu kuwake 郵便の種類別区分け mail merge
yūbin-posuto 郵便ポスト mail box
yūjin no 有人の manned
yūka-shōken 有価証券

securities
yūka-shōken-ichiranhyō 有価証券一覧表 brand portfolio, stock portfolio
yūkei-shisan 有形資産 tangible assets
yūkei-zaisan 有形財産 tangible assets
yūkiteki-seichō 有機的成長 organic growth
yūkō 有効 efficient
yūkōsei 有効性 effectiveness
yūkyū-seisan-nōryoku 遊休生産能力 idle capacity
yūkyū-shisetsu 遊休施設 idle facilities
yūro-darā ユーロダラー Eurodollar
yūro-manē ユーロマネー Eurocurrency
yūro-sai ユーロ債 Eurobond
yūryō-kabu 優良株 blue-chip, gilt-edged stock
yūsen-jun'i o bapponteki ni minaoshite sakusei-shita yosan 優先順位を抜本的に見直して作成した予算 zero-base budget
yūsenken o ataeru 優先権を与える prioritize *v.*

Z

zaiko-kaiten-ritsu 在庫回転率 inventory turnover
zaiko (hin)-kanri 在庫（品）管理 inventory control, stock control
zaikohin no kaiten-ritsu 在庫品の回転率 stock turnover
zaikohin-hyōka 在庫品評価 stock valuation
zaikohin-kaiten-ritsu 在庫品回転率 stock turnover, inventory turnover
zaikohin-shirabe 在庫品調べ stocktaking
zaimu 財務 financial administration
zaimu-bunseki 財務分析 financial analysis
zaimu-hiritsu 財務比率 financial ratio
zaimu-hoshō 財務保証 financial guarantee
zaimu-jōkyō 財務状況 financial position
zaimu-jōkyō no gaiyō 財務状況の概要 financial review
zaimu-jōtai 財務状態 financial position
zaimu-kanri 財務管理 financial administration, financial control, financial management
zaimu-keikaku 財務計画 financial planning
zaimu-kijun 財務基準 financial standards
zaimu-minaoshi 財務見直し financial review
zaimu-satei 財務査定 financial appraisal
zaimu-sekininsha 財務責任者 financial director
zaimu-senryaku 財務戦略 financial strategy
zaimu-shohyō 財務諸表 financial statement
zaimu-tantō-torishimariyaku 財務担当取締役 financial director
zaisei-seisaku 財政政策 fiscal policy
zaisei-senryaku 財政戦略 financial strategy
zaiseiteki-shigeki 財政的刺激 financial incentive
zaiteku 財テク zaitech
zangyō 残業 overtime
zappi 雑費 petty expenses
zeisei-jō no yūgū-sochi 税制上の優遇措置 tax incentive
zeigaku-satei-jimusho 税額査定事務所 assessment centre
zeikin-kōjo 税金控除 tax deductible
zen-seisan-kōtei no hoshu 全生産工程の保守 total plant maintenance
zenchikyūteki-imēji 全地球的イメージ global image
zenmenteki na 全面的な down the line
zennōryoku 全能力 full capacity
zensha-moderu 全社モデル corporate model
zentai-genka-keisan 全体原価計算 absorption costing

zentaiteki-hinshitsu-kanri 全体的品質管理 total quality managemnt (TQM)
zero-hyōka ゼロ評価 zero-rating
zero-samu-gēmu ゼロサムゲーム zero-sum game
zetto-ẓuhyō Z図表 Z chart
zōbun-genkin-furō 増分現金フロー incremental cash flow
zōbun-genkin-ryūdō 増分現金流動 incremental cash flow
zōbun-genkin-shūshi 増分現金収支 incremental cash flow
zōka-bun no 増加分の incremental
zukei 図形 graphics
zushiki-shiyōsha-intāfēsu 図式使用者インターフェース graphical user interface (GUI)